Betty Crocker's
QUICK DINNERS
IN 30 MINUTES OR LESS

PRENTICE HALL

New York   London   Toronto   Sydney   Tokyo   Singapore

PRENTICE HALL GENERAL REFERENCE
15 Columbus Circle
New York, New York, 10023

Library of Congress Cataloging-in-Publication Data

Crocker, Betty.
   [Quick dinners]
   Betty Crocker's quick dinners.
      p.   cm.
   Includes index.
   ISBN 0-671-84692-2
   1. Dinners and dining. 2. Quick and easy cookery.
   I. Title. II. Title: Quick dinners.
TX737.C72 1993
641.5'55—dc20   92-25396
                                           CIP

Designed by Levavi & Levavi, Inc.
Manufactured in the United States of America

10 9 8 7 6 5 4 3 2 1

First Edition

Front cover: Quick Jambalaya (page 56)
Back cover: Pork Chops with Rhubarb Sauce (page 16)

Contents

Introduction   iv

Meal-Planning Pointers   v

1. **Meat Express**   1

2. **Pleasing Poultry**   23

3. **Speedy Fish and Seafood**   41

4. **Meatless Meals**   63

Index   77

Introduction

Everyone seems to be looking for quick, nutritious and delicious meals today. Even though time is limited, our desire for great taste isn't, and with *Betty Crocker's Quick Dinners*, you'll discover more than 100 main dishes that satisfy all your time and taste requirements—in 30 minutes or less!

In the mood for a chicken main dish? Sample Spicy Chicken with Broccoli or Chicken Breasts in Mustard Sauce. Thinking about fish or shellfish? Try Mediterranean-style Sole, Shrimp Fajitas or Stir-fried Scallops and Pea Pods. When you'd like a main dish with meat, try Chile Burgers, Quick Lasagne or Pork and Broccoli Risotto. And when you prefer a meatless meal, you'll enjoy Southwestern Eggs, Tortellini in Balsamic Vinaigrette or Bean and Cheese Tacos.

In addition to these appealing—and speedy—recipes, you'll find tips throughout the book to help you create great meals in almost no time, including menus to help plan meals easily. *Betty Crocker's Quick Dinners* is the answer to what to make for dinner when you are pressed for time; however, we think you'll find these recipes so good you'll make them any time, not only when you are trying to beat the clock.

THE BETTY CROCKER EDITORS

Meal-Planning Pointers

In addition to the recipes here, there are other easy ideas to help you beat the clock. Try the following to speed you dinner along.

- Read the recipe completely and assemble all the ingredients and equipment before starting to cook.
- Plan for leftovers, to make a second meal quick and easy.
- When possible, make double portions of favorite dishes and freeze or refrigerate half for later.
- Try roasting two types of meat at the same time, for example, chicken and beef. Serve one hot that night and save the other to serve hot or cold the next day.
- Pair foods that can cook in the same pan or at the same oven temperature.
- When you have time prepare such staples as toasted coconut, toasted nuts, dry bread crumbs and croutons. Cover tightly and store for future use.
- Keep store-bought frozen chopped onion on hand, or make your own: Place peeled, chopped onion in boiling water about 1½ minutes. Chill immediately in ice water. Drain, package and freeze.
- If you forget to chill canned fruits or vegetables, give them a quick chill in the freezer for twenty minutes.
- When you want to save even more preparation time, use ingredients from your deli or a salad bar. Use cut-up vegetables for salads, crudités, a stir-fry or in specific recipes. A deli is an excellent source for prepared salads and cooked meats.
- Store-bought tomatoes are generally hard and need time to ripen, so always try to keep a few on hand so they'll be ripe when you want them. Tomatoes are wonderful when added to a salad, sliced and served as a side dish, and finely chopped and mixed with plain yogurt, sour cream or mayonnaise for a meat or vegetable sauce.
- Use your microwave to cook one item of a meal while you prepare the rest conventionally. Vegetables are excellent cooked in a microwave; the microwave is also great to whip up a fast dessert of "baked" fruit. (See Microwaving Fresh Vegetables, page xii.)
- Get family and friends involved in meal preparation. Parcel out chopping, salad making, beverage detail, table setting, even answering the phone. Meal preparation will go more quickly, and you'll enjoy the company.

HOW TO USE NUTRITION INFORMATION

Nutrition information per serving for each recipe includes the amounts of calories, protein, carbohydrate, fat, cholesterol, and sodium.

- If ingredient choices are given, the first listed ingredient is used in recipe nutrition information calculations.
- When ingredient ranges or more than one serving size is indicated, the first weight or serving is used to calculate nutrition information.
- "If desired" ingredients and recipe variations are not included in nutrition information calculations.

Serving Ideas

With very little effort you can trim even more time off preparing your dinners—and use leftovers creatively—with the tips below.

• Take leftovers from one meal and make them into a different dish. Try these ideas:

Cut leftover meat into small pieces and toss with salad greens and a tangy horseradish or mustard dressing for a refreshing salad.

Change the flavor of gravy and sauces by adding different herbs and spices.

Turn plain baked or boiled potatoes into a potato salad. Toss with a vinaigrette dressing instead of mayonnaise for a new flavor. Toss with a low-calorie vinaigrette if you'd like to save calories.

When you cook pasta, double the amount. Toss half with olive oil, cover and refrigerate. You'll have the beginnings of a pasta salad for the following night.

Use leftover vegetables in omeletes or salads.

Perk up sandwiches with horseradish, chiles or flavored mustards.

• Plain yogurt can become a side dish, sauce or dessert when it's mixed with one of the following:

Sliced cucumber for a quick, cooling cucumber salad

Hot vegetables, cracked pepper and parsley for a side dish

Shredded or finely chopped cucumber and dill weed as a sauce for fish or chicken

Tarragon for a vegetable or meat sauce

Fresh fruit, then sprinkled with brown sugar or honey for a dessert

• Make seasoned butters to jazz up plain vegetables. Heat ¼ cup butter or margarine over low heat until melted, then mix in one of the following ingredients:

2 tablespoons grated Parmesan cheese
¼ teaspoon curry powder
1 tablespoon prepared horseradish
1 tablespoon sesame seeds and 2 tablespoons soy sauce
1 clove garlic, finely chopped

• Top bread slices, English muffins, corn bread or frankfurter buns with flavored butters or shredded or grated cheese and broil until bubbly.

• Mix ½ cup margarine or butter with 1 teaspoon dried thyme, dill weed or basil. Cover and store in the refrigerator to use for a quick bread topping.

Microwaving Fresh Vegetables

Microwaves are a wonderful way to cook fresh vegetables quickly. The guide below will tell you exactly how to microwave your vegetables.

For whole, wash and pierce in several places allowing steam to escape. For pieces, wash, trim and pare as necessary; cut into pieces about the same size.

Place vegetables with larger, denser parts toward the outside edge of a microwave casserole dish. For whole potatoes or unhusked corn, place uncovered (potatoes in circle) on paper towel in microwave; let stand uncovered.

Add water as directed. Cover tightly and microwave on high until crisp-tender or tender, stirring, rotating casserole, turning over or rearranging food as directed. Let stand covered.

TYPE	AMOUNT	WATER	TIME (high)	STAND TIME
Asparagus				
spears	1½ pounds	¼ cup	6 to 9 min, rotating dish ½ turn after 3 min	1 min
pieces, 1 inch	1½ pounds	¼ cup	6 to 9 min, stirring after 3 min	1 min
Beans—Green, Wax				
pieces, 1 inch	1 pound	½ cup	9 to 14 min, stirring after 5 min	5 min
Broccoli				
spears	1½ pounds	1 cup	9 to 12 min, rotating dish ½ turn ever 4 min	5 min
pieces, 1 inch	1½ pounds	1 cup	9 to 12 min, stirring every 9 min	5 min
Brussels Sprouts	1 pound	¼ cup	8 to 13 min, stirring after 5 min	5 min
Cabbage—Green, Red, Savoy				
wedges	1 pound	½ cup	10 to 14 min, rotating dish ½ turn after 5 min	5 min
shredded	1 pound	¼ cup	8 to 10 min, stirring after 4 min	5 min
Carrots				
slices, ¼ inch	1 pound	¼ cup	6 to 8 min, stirring after 4 min	1 min

TYPE	AMOUNT	WATER	TIME (high)	STAND TIME
Cauliflower				
whole	2 pounds	¼ cup	12 to 14 min, rotating dish ½ turn after 6 min	1 min
cauliflowerets	2 pounds	¼ cup	12 to 14 min, stirring after 6 min	1 min
Corn				
husked	4 ears	¼ cup	9 to 14 min, rearranging after 5 min	5 min
unhusked	4 ears	—	9 to 14 min, rearranging after 5 min	5 min
Peas, Green	2 pounds	¼ cup	9 to 11 min, stirring after 5 min	1 min
Potatoes, White				
whole (4)	2 pounds	—	12 to 18 min, turning over after 6 min	5 min
pieces	2 pounds	½ cup	10 to 16 min, stirring after 7 min	1 min
Potatoes, Sweet (Yams)	1½ pounds	—	8 to 15 min, turning over after 4 min	5 min
Summer Squash— Crookneck, Pattypan, Straightneck, Zucchini				
slices or cubes	1½ pounds	¼ cup	8 to 10 min, stirring after 4 min	1 min
Winter Squash— Acorn, Buttercup, Butternut				
whole or piece	2 pounds	—	4 to 6 min or until rind is easy to cut through; cut in half, microwave 5 to 8 min longer	1 min

Defrosting Poultry, Seafood and Meats

Microwaves also give you a jump on cooking by allowing you to defrost poultry, seafood, and meats quickly and safely. Follow the guide below to defrost easily and accurately.

Defrost in microwavable wrapper or place in shallow microwavable dish. Pierce tightly closed packages, allowing steam to escape. Cover seafood. After half the time, separate, turn over, break up or rearrange in dish. Arrange thickest parts to outside edge if possible.

Microwave on defrost setting as directed until few ice crystals remain in center. Edges should not begin to cook. Let stand 5 to 15 minutes to complete defrosting.

POULTRY

TYPE	AMOUNT	TIME (defrost)
Chicken Broiler-fryer, cut up	3 to 3½ pounds	20 to 25 min, turning over and separating every 10 min
Breast halves (2), with skin and bones	1¼ pounds	12 to 15 min, turning over and separating after 8 min
Breast halves (4), skinless, boneless	1½ pounds	15 to 20 min, turning over and separating after 10 min
Drumsticks, thighs and wings	2 pounds	12 to 15 min, separating after 8 min
Turkey Tenderloins (2)	1½ pounds	10 to 12 min, separating and turning over after 5 min
Breast slices	1 pound	8 to 10 min, separating and turning over after 4 min
Rock Cornish hen (1)	1½ pounds	10 to 12 min, turning over after 5 min; let stand 30 min in cold water

SEAFOOD

TYPE	AMOUNT	TIME (defrost)
Fish fillets, ½ to ¾ inch	1 pound	6 to 8 min, separating and rearranging after 3 min
Fish steaks (2), 1 inch	1 pound	6 to 8 min, separating and rearranging after 3 min
Crabmeat	6 to 8 ounces	4 to 7 min, breaking up after 2 min
Lobster tails (4)	2 pounds	8 to 10 min, rotating dish ½ turn after 5 min
Scallops	1 pound	8 to 10 min, stirring after 4 min
Shrimp, in shells or peeled and deveined	1 pound	6 to 8 min, stirring after 3 min

MEATS—Beef, Veal, Pork, Lamb

TYPE	AMOUNT	TIME (defrost)
Steaks, ½ to 1 inch	1 pound	7 to 11 min, separating and turning over after 4 min
Chops (4), ½ inch	1 pound	6 to 9 min, separating and rearranging after 4 min
Ribs, back	1 pound	7 to 9 min, separating and rearranging after 4 min
Ground bulk	1 pound	8 to 10 min, breaking up and removing thawed meat after 4 min
patties (4), ¾ inch	1 pound	8 to 10 min, separating and turning over after 4 min
Bacon, sliced	1 pound	5 to 6 min
Frankfurters (10)	1 pound	5 to 7 min, turning over after 3 min
Sausages (6), uncooked or cooked (bratwurst, Italian, Polish)	1 pound	6 to 8 min, turning over after 3 min

Stocking the Kitchen

A well-stocked pantry and the right cooking equipment guarantee hours saved. The right tool for the right job will keep your cooking easy and efficient. And knowing that basic ingredients are right inside your cupboard will allow you to assemble one meal after another in minutes.

Below are guidelines for stocking your kitchen. We have not listed common pantry items, since you know what items you use on a regular basis. Rather, these are general guidelines to use in addition to the kitchen equipment and shopping knowledge you already have.

EQUIPMENT

No doubt you have basic kitchen equipment and know how to use it. To cut down on cooking time, you may want to use a microwave and a food processor; both are readily available in a selection of price ranges.

- Always keep knives sharpened; cutting will be faster and safer.
- Use nonstick cookware and bakeware; they eliminate the need for greasing and are easier to clean.
- Use the correct utensils to measure ingredients. Use a glass measuring cup for liquids; graduated, nested measuring cups for dry ingredients and solid fats; graduated measuring spoons for both dry and liquid ingredients.
- Use the proper equipment for the task; pare vegetables with a vegetable parer, use a colander to drain pasta, kitchen shears to cut poultry or snip herbs, a basting brush for basting, a kitchen timer to keep track of cooking times and so on. If you don't have the basics, it's worth the modest investment to stock your kitchen properly.

A Week of Menus

FAMILY DINNER
Easy Tacos (page 8)
Fresh Fruit Salad
Milk
Cookies

HEARTY DINNER
Quick Lasagne (page 8)
Tossed Green Salad
Garlic Bread
Hot Chocolate
Brownies

SPEEDY COMPANY DINNER
Shrimp Étouffée (page 54)
Hot Rice
Cole Slaw
Make-your-own Ice Cream Sundaes
Coffee and Tea

ON THE GRILL
Grilled Meatball Kabobs (page 12)
Grilled Zucchini and Corn on the Cob
Sliced Cucumbers and Tomatoes
Cold Watermelon
Ice Tea

INTERNATIONAL FLAVOR
Spicy Chicken with Broccoli (page 26)
Hot Cooked Rice
Fortune Cookies and Sliced Pineapple
Tea

LAZY DAY DINNER
Turkey Slices with Walnuts (page 34)
Dinner Rolls
Steamed Green Beans
Grapes and Cookies
Milk

SIMPLY SALAD
Raspberry–Chicken Salad (page 31)
Potato Salad
Cut-up Fresh Vegetables
Sorbet or Sherbet with Berries
Lemonade

1

Meat Express

=■=

London Broil

Nice with a tossed salad and boiled new potatoes.

1 pound high-quality beef flank steak
1 tablespoon margarine or butter
2 medium onions, thinly sliced
¼ teaspoon salt
2 tablespoons vegetable oil
1 teaspoon lemon juice
½ teaspoon salt
¼ teaspoon pepper
2 cloves garlic, crushed

Cut both sides of beef steak in diamond pattern ⅛ inch deep. Heat margarine in 10-inch skillet over medium-high heat. Sauté onions and ¼ teaspoon salt in margarine about 4 minutes or until light brown; keep warm. Mix remaining ingredients; brush half of the mixture over beef.

Set oven control to broil. Broil beef with top 2 to 3 inches from heat about 5 minutes or until brown. Turn beef; brush with remaining oil mixture. Broil 5 minutes longer. Cut beef across grain at slanted angle into thin slices; serve with onions.   **4 servings**

PER SERVING: Calories 260; Protein 24 g; Carbohydrate 6 g; Fat 15 g; Cholesterol 70 mg; Sodium 480 mg

Sweet and Sour Beef

1 pound beef flank steak
3 tablespoons vegetable oil
1 medium onion, cut into 1-inch pieces
1 can (8 ounces) pineapple chunks in juice, undrained
¼ cup sugar
¼ cup white vinegar
1 tablespoon instant chicken bouillon
1 tablespoon soy sauce
1 tablespoon cornstarch
1 tablespoon cold water
1 medium green bell pepper, cut into 1-inch pieces
2 medium tomatoes, cut into eighths

Cut beef with grain into 2-inch strips. Cut strips across grain into ⅛-inch slices.

Heat oil in 12-inch skillet or wok over medium-high heat until hot. Add beef and onion; cook and stir until beef is brown, about 3 minutes. Stir in pineapple, sugar, vinegar, bouillon (dry) and soy sauce. Heat to boiling.

Mix cornstarch and cold water; stir into beef mixture. Cook and stir 1 minute. Stir in bell pepper and tomatoes; cook and stir 1 minute. Serve with hot cooked rice if desired.   **5 servings**

PER SERVING: Calories 315; Protein 21 g; Carbohydrate 24 g; Fat 15 g; Cholesterol 50 mg; Sodium 270 mg

Beef–Orange Stir-Fry

Beef–Orange Stir-Fry

To cut beef more easily, partially freeze beef about 1 hour.

- 1 pound boneless sirloin steak
- 4 medium stalks bok choy
- 2 medium carrots
- 1 tablespoon vegetable oil
- 1 teaspoon ground ginger
- 2 medium cloves garlic, chopped
- 2 tablespoons vegetable oil
- 1 package (6 ounces) frozen pea pods, thawed slightly
- 1 small onion, chopped (about ¼ cup)
- 1 cup orange juice
- ½ cup cold water
- 2 tablespoons cornstarch
- 2 tablespoons soy sauce
- ⅛ teaspoon crushed red pepper
- Hot cooked rice

Trim fat from beef steak. Cut beef with grain into thin 2-inch strips. Cut bok choy diagonally into ¼-inch slices; chop the green tops. Cut carrots diagonally into thin slices. Heat 12-inch skillet or wok until 1 or 2 drops of water bubble and skitter when sprinkled in skillet.

Add 1 tablespoon oil; rotate skillet to coat side. Add beef and sprinkle with ginger and garlic. Cook and stir about 3 minutes or until beef is brown. Remove beef from skillet.

Add 2 tablespoons oil to skillet; rotate skillet to coat side. Add bok choy, carrots, pea pods and onion. Cook and stir about 3 minutes or until carrots are tender. Stir in beef and orange juice; heat to boiling. Mix cold water, cornstarch, soy sauce and red pepper; stir into beef mixture. Cook and stir about 1 minute or until thickened. Serve over hot cooked rice.   **4 servings**

PER SERVING: Calories 345; Protein 32 g; Carbohydrate 20 g; Fat 15 g; Cholesterol 75 mg; Sodium 600 mg

Curried Beef with Fruit

- 1 package (8 ounces) mixed dried fruit
- 2½ cups boiling water
- 3 teaspoons curry powder
- ½ teaspoon salt
- 2 cloves garlic, finely chopped
- 2 tablespoons margarine or butter
- 2 tablespoons cornstarch
- ¼ cup orange juice
- ¾ cup orange juice
- 3 cups cut-up cooked roast beef
- 6 green onions, cut into 1-inch pieces
- 3 cups hot cooked rice
- ⅓ cup slivered almonds

Remove pits from prunes. Pour boiling water over fruit; let stand. Cook curry powder, salt and garlic in margarine in 3-quart saucepan over medium heat 5 minutes, stirring occasionally. Mix cornstarch and ¼ cup orange juice. Stir cornstarch mixture, ¾ cup orange juice and the fruit (with liquid) into curry mixture. Heat to boiling, stirring constantly. Boil and stir 1 minute. Stir in beef and onions; heat until hot. Serve over rice. Sprinkle with almonds.   **6 servings**

PER SERVING: Calories 480; Protein 28 g; Carbohydrate 66 g; Fat 12 g; Cholesterol 65 mg; Sodium 670 mg

Quick Beef Dinner

Simple, satisfying and hearty.

1 pound ground beef
2 stalks celery, sliced (about 1 cup)
1 medium onion, chopped (about ½ cup)
1 clove garlic, minced
1 can (16 ounces) whole kernel corn, undrained
1 can (16 ounces) pork and beans
½ cup chopped green bell pepper
1 teaspoon salt
1 can (6 ounces) tomato paste

Cook and stir meat, celery, onion and garlic in large skillet until meat is brown. Drain off fat. Stir in corn (with liquid) and remaining ingredients.

Heat mixture to boiling. Reduce heat; cover and simmer 10 minutes, stirring occasionally.

6 servings

PER SERVING: Calories 350; Protein 21 g; Carbohydrate 37 g; Fat 13 g; Cholesterol 50 mg; Sodium 1,210 mg

Easy Hot Dish

1 pound ground beef
1 medium onion, chopped (about ½ cup)
1 can (8 ounces) whole kernel corn, undrained
1 can (8 ounces) tomato sauce
¼ cup halved pitted ripe olives
4 ounces uncooked noodles (about 2 cups)
2 cups water
1 teaspoon dried oregano leaves
½ teaspoon salt
¼ teaspoon pepper
1 cup shredded Cheddar cheese (4 ounces)

Cook and stir meat and onion in large skillet until meat is brown. Drain off fat. Stir in corn (with liquid) and remaining ingredients.

Heat mixture to boiling. Reduce heat and simmer uncovered, stirring occasionally, until noodles are tender, about 20 minutes.

6 servings

PER SERVING: Calories 360; Protein 23 g; Carbohydrate 24 g; Fat 19 g; Cholesterol 80 mg; Sodium 740 mg

Double-Cheese Hamburger Skillet

A fun twist on the classic cheeseburger.

4 ounces uncooked egg noodles (about 2 cups)
1 pound ground beef
⅓ cup chopped onion
¼ cup chopped celery
1 can (8 ounces) tomato sauce
1 teaspoon salt
1 package (3 ounces) cream cheese, softened
½ cup creamed cottage cheese
¼ cup sour cream
1 medium tomato, if desired

Cook noodles as directed on package; drain. While noodles are cooking, cook and stir meat, onion and celery in large skillet until meat is brown. Drain off fat. Stir in noodles, tomato sauce, salt, cream cheese, cottage cheese and sour cream.

Heat mixture to boiling. Reduce heat and simmer uncovered 5 minutes, stirring frequently. Remove from heat. Cut tomato into thin slices and arrange on meat mixture. Cover until tomato slices are warm, about 5 minutes.

5 servings

PER SERVING: Calories 395; Protein 25 g; Carbohydrate 22 g; Fat 23 g; Cholesterol 100 mg; Sodium 990 mg

Spaghetti and Beef Sauce

1 pound ground beef
1 large onion, chopped (about 1 cup)
1 clove garlic, crushed
1 teaspoon sugar
1 teaspoon dried oregano leaves
3/4 teaspoon salt
3/4 teaspoon dried basil leaves
1/2 teaspoon dried marjoram leaves
1 can (16 ounces) whole tomatoes,
  undrained
1 can (8 ounces) tomato sauce
4 cups hot cooked spaghetti

Cook and stir ground beef, onion and garlic in 10-inch skillet until beef is light brown; drain. Stir in remaining ingredients except spaghetti; break up tomatoes. Heat to boiling; reduce heat. Cover and simmer, stirring occasionally, 1 hour. Serve over spaghetti and, if desired, with grated Parmesan cheese.   **6 servings**

PER SERVING: Calories 330; Protein 20 g; Carbohydrate 36 g; Fat 12 g; Cholesterol 45 mg; Sodium 790 mg

Broiled Burgers with Mushrooms and Onions

1 pound ground beef
3 tablespoons finely chopped onion
3 tablespoons water
3/4 teaspoon salt
1/8 teaspoon pepper
Mushrooms and Onions (right)

Mix ground beef, onion, water, salt and pepper. Shape mixture into 4 patties, each about 3/4 inch thick.

Set oven control to broil. Place patties on rack in broiler pan. Broil with tops about 3 inches from heat until desired doneness, 5 to 7 minutes on each side for medium. Prepare Mushrooms and Onions; spoon over hamburgers.   **4 servings**

PER SERVING: Calories 280; Protein 22 g; Carbohydrate 5 g; Fat 19 g; Cholesterol 65 mg; Sodium 610 mg

Mushrooms and Onions

1 medium onion, thinly sliced
1 tablespoon margarine or butter
1 can (4 ounces) mushroom stems and
  pieces, drained
1/2 teaspoon Worcestershire sauce

Cook onion in margarine over medium heat, stirring occasionally, until tender. Stir in mushrooms and Worcestershire sauce; heat until mushrooms are hot.

TO GRILL: Prepare patties as directed above. Grill patties about 4 inches from medium coals, turning once, until desired doneness, 7 to 8 minutes on each side for medium.

MICROWAVE DIRECTIONS: Prepare patties as directed above. Place patties on microwavable rack in microwavable dish. Cover with waxed paper and microwave on high (100%) 3 minutes; rotate dish 1/2 turn. Microwave until almost done, about 2 minutes longer. Let stand covered 3 minutes.

Place onion and margarine in 1-quart microwavable casserole. Cover tightly and microwave on high (100%) until onion is crisp-tender, about 2 minutes. Stir in mushrooms and Worcestershire sauce. Cover tightly and microwave until mushrooms are hot, about 1 minutes. Spoon over hamburgers.

Chile Burgers

This is also very good with regular ground beef.

1½ **pounds lean ground beef**
1 **egg**
1 **can (4 ounces) chopped green chiles, drained**
½ **cup finely crushed corn chips**
1 **small onion, chopped (about ¼ cup)**
1 **medium clove garlic, crushed**
1 **tablespoon chile powder**
2 **medium tomatoes, each cut into 4 slices**
1 **cup shredded Monterey Jack cheese (4 ounces)**

Mix all ingredients except tomatoes and cheese. Shape mixture into 8 patties, each about ½ inch thick. Place patties on rack in broiler pan. Set oven control to broil. Broil patties with tops about 3 inches from heat, 5 to 7 minutes on each side or until medium doneness. Place 1 tomato slice on each patty. Sprinkle each with 2 tablespoons cheese. Broil about 2 minutes or just until cheese is melted. **8 servings**

PER SERVING: Calories 210; Protein 26 g; Carbohydrate 4 g; Fat 10 g; Cholesterol 90 mg; Sodium 155 mg

Grilled Teriyaki Burgers

1 **pound ground beef**
2 **tablespoons soy sauce**
1 **teaspoon salt**
¼ **teaspoon crushed gingerroot or**
⅛ **teaspoon ground ginger**
1 **clove garlic, crushed**

Shape ground beef into 4 patties, each about ¾ inch thick. Mix remaining ingredients; spoon onto patties Turn patties. Let stand 10 minutes.

Grill patties about 4 inches from medium coals, turning once, until desired doneness, 5 to 7 minutes on each side for medium. Serve on toasted sesame seed buns if desired. **4 servings**

PER SERVING: Calories 230; Protein 21 g; Carbohydrate 1 g; Fat 16 g; Cholesterol 65 mg; Sodium 1,100 mg

TO BROIL: Prepare patties as directed above. Set oven control to broil. Place patties on rack in broiler pan. Broil with tops about 3 inches from heat, turning once, until desired doneness, about 5 minutes on each side for medium. Serve on toasted sesame seed buns if desired.

Burger Bar

Half the fun of eating a hamburger is in the "fixings," the condiments that go with it. Try the toppings below to add zip to your burgers:

Barbecue sauce
Blue cheese dressing
Cheese slices
Chile sauce
Chutney
Horseradish sauce
Ketchup
Mayonnaise
Mustard
Pickle relish
Worcestershire sauce
Alfalfa sprouts
Avocado slices
Bell pepper rings
Cooked bacon
Coleslaw
Onion slices
Pickles (sweet and sour)
Shredded lettuce
Sliced mushrooms
Tomato slices

Grilled Teriyaki Burgers

Easy Tacos

You can also put meat mixture into pre-pared taco shells, if you like, and omit tortilla chips. Top with the remaining ingredients.

  1 pound ground beef
  1 large onion, chopped (about 1 cup)
  1 envelope (about 1¼ ounces) taco seasoning mix
  1 cup water
  1 package (12 ounces) tortilla chips
  ½ head lettuce, shredded
  2 medium tomatoes, chopped
  1 can (2¼ ounces) sliced ripe olives, drained
  1 cup shredded Cheddar or Monterey Jack cheese (4 ounces)
  ⅔ cup sour cream

Cook and stir ground beef and onion in 10-inch skillet until beef is brown; drain. Stir in seasoning mix (dry) and water.

Heat to boiling; reduce heat. Simmer uncovered 10 minutes, stirring occasionally. Spoon beef mixture onto chips. Top with remaining ingredients.   **6 servings**

PER SERVING: Calories 600; Protein 25 g; Carbohydrate 46 g; Fat 35 g; Cholesterol 80 mg; Sodium 970 mg

MICROWAVE DIRECTIONS: Crumble ground beef into 2-quart microwavable casserole; add onion. Cover loosely and microwave on high 3 minutes; break up beef and stir. Cover loosely and microwave until very little pink remains in beef, 2 to 5 minutes longer; drain.

Stir in seasoning mix (dry) and ¾ cup water. Microwave uncovered on high 3 minutes; stir. Microwave uncovered until hot, 2 to 5 minutes longer. Continue as directed above.

Quick Lasagne

Instant lasagne noodles let you make homemade lasagne any night you're in the mood, not just when you have extra time.

  ½ pound ground beef
  1 medium clove garlic, chopped
  1 teaspoon Italian seasoning
  1 cup spaghetti sauce
  6 uncooked instant lasagne noodles (each about 6½ × 3 inches)
  1 container (12 ounces) low-fat cottage cheese
  1 cup shredded Monterey Jack cheese (4 ounces)
  2 tablespoons grated Parmesan cheese

Heat oven to 400°. Cook ground beef and garlic in 10-inch skillet over medium heat, stirring frequently, until ground beef is brown; drain. Stir in Italian seasoning and spaghetti sauce. Heat to boiling; remove from heat.

Spread ¼ cup beef mixture in square pan, 8 × 8 × 2 or 9 × 9 × 2 inches. Top with 2 lasagne noodles. Spread one-third of the beef mixture (about ½ cup) over noodles in pan. Spread one-third of the cottage cheese (about ½ cup) over beef mixture.

Sprinkle with one-third of the Monterey Jack cheese (about ⅓ cup) on top. Repeat layering twice. Sprinkle with Parmesan cheese. Bake about 10 minutes or until hot and cheese is melted. Let stand 5 minutes before serving.

4 servings

PER SERVING: Calories 470; Protein 35 g; Carbohydrate 33 g; Fat 22 g; Cholesterol 70 mg; Sodium 1,000 mg

Quick Lasagne

Veal with Spinach and Fettuccine

¾ **pound thin slices lean veal round steak or veal for scallopini**
1 **cup sliced fresh mushrooms (about 3 ounces)**
¼ **cup chopped shallots**
½ **cup Madeira wine or beef broth**
½ **cup beef broth**
2 **teaspoons cornstarch**
⅛ **teaspoon pepper**
1 **package (10 ounces) frozen chopped spinach, thawed and well drained**
2 **cups hot cooked fettuccine**

Cut veal crosswise into ¼-inch strips. Spray 10-inch nonstick skillet with nonstick cooking spray. Sauté veal, mushrooms and shallots in skillet over medium-high heat 3 to 5 minutes or until veal is done. Mix wine, broth, cornstarch and pepper. Stir wine mixture and spinach into skillet. Heat to boiling, stirring constantly. Boil and stir 1 minute. Serve over fettuccine.

4 servings

PER SERVING: Calories 255; Protein 20 g; Carbohydrate 23 g; Fat 7 g; Cholesterol 55 mg; Sodium 190 mg

MICROWAVE DIRECTIONS: Decrease wine to ⅓ cup. Trim fat from veal. Cut veal crosswise into ¼-inch strips. Place veal, mushrooms and shallots in 2-quart microwavable casserole. Cover and microwave on high 5 to 6 minutes, stirring every 2 minutes, until veal is done; drain. Mix wine, broth, cornstarch and pepper. Stir wine mixture and spinach into casserole. Cover and microwave 4 to 5 minutes, stirring every 2 minutes, until thickened.

Ground Meat Storage Freezing and Defrosting Tips

Ground meat often goes on sale, and it makes good economic sense to stock up. Just follow these easy guidelines to freeze and defrost meat.

• If you have a large package of ground meat, divide it into smaller packets to make thawing time shorter.

• Layer ground meat patties between double sheets of freezer wrap so they separate easily, or freeze a single layer on cookie sheets, then transfer to freezer bags. This way patties won't stick together, and you can use as many as you need at one time.

• Always label your packages, and write the date by which the meat must be used. Ground meat should not be stored in the freezer longer than 4 months. You can also add any special reheating instructions, or additional ingredients that will be needed before serving.

• When defrosting ground meat, transfer it to the refrigerator the night before you plan to use it, so that it will be defrosted by the next evening. As a general rule, 1 pound of ground meat will thaw in approximately 24 hours.

• Never defrost ground meat at room temperature as it gives harmful bacteria the chance to grow and make the meat unsafe to eat.

• Use meat as soon as possible after defrosting—never refreeze defrosted ground meat.

Veal with Spinach and Fettuccine

Grilled Meatball Kabobs

1 pound ground beef, pork and veal
   mixture
1 tablespoon chopped fresh parsley
1 tablespoon chopped fresh basil leaves
1 teaspoon salt
1 teaspoon pepper
1 small onion, finely chopped (about 1/4
   cup)
2 cloves garlic, finely chopped
1 egg
1 large green bell pepper, cut into 1-inch
   squares

Mix all ingredients except bell pepper. Shape mixture into 1-inch balls. Alternate meatballs and bell-pepper squares on each of four 12-inch metal skewers, leaving space between each meatball and bell-pepper square. Cover and grill kabobs about 4 inches from hot coals 10 minutes, turning frequently, until meat is done.

4 servings

PER SERVING: Calories 295; Protein 23 g; Carbohydrate 17 g; Fat 15 g; Cholesterol 145 mg; Sodium 830 mg

BROILED MEATBALL KABOBS: Set oven control to broil. Place kabobs on rack in broiler pan. Broil with tops about 3 inches from heat 5 minutes. Turn kabobs. Broil 4 to 5 minutes longer or until meat is done.

Burger Beef Soup

1 pound ground beef
1 small onion, chopped (about 1/4 cup)
2 cups tomato juice
1 1/4 cups water
1 can (10 3/4 ounces) condensed cream of
   celery soup
3/4 teaspoon chopped fresh or 1/4 teaspoon dried basil leaves
3/4 teaspoon chopped fresh or 1/4 teaspoon dried marjoram leaves
1/8 teaspoon pepper
1 bay leaf
1/2 cup frozen peas
2 ounces uncooked egg noodles (1 cup)

Cook ground beef and onion in 4-quart Dutch oven over medium heat about 10 minutes, stirring frequently, or until beef is brown; drain. Stir in remaining ingredients except noodles. Heat to boiling. Stir in noodles; reduce heat. Simmer uncovered about 10 minutes, stirring occasionally, until noodles are tender. Remove bay leaf.

4 servings

PER SERVING: Calories 425; Protein 27 g; Carbohydrate 32 g; Fat 21 g; Cholesterol 95 mg; Sodium 1,090 mg

Lamb Chops with Pineapple

The fresh-tasting combination of mint and pineapple complements lamb beautifully.

3 tablespoons orange juice
2 tablespoons honey
4 lamb loin chops, 1 inch thick (about
  1 pound)
1½ cups cubed pineapple
1 tablespoon chopped fresh or 1 teaspoon dried mint leaves

Set oven control to broil. Mix orange juice and honey; reserve 2 tablespoons. Place lamb chops on rack in broiler pan. Brush lamb with reserved orange mixture. Broil with tops about 5 inches from heat about 6 minutes or until brown; turn. Brush with reserved orange mixture. Broil 6 to 9 minutes or until desired doneness.

Heat remaining orange mixture, the pineapple and mint to boiling, stirring occasionally. Serve with lamb chops.   **4 servings**

PER SERVING: Calories 425; Protein 19 g; Carbohydrate 28 g; Fat 26 g; Cholesterol 85 mg; Sodium 50 mg

NOTE: 1 can (20 ounces) pineapple chunks, drained, can be substituted for the fresh pineapple.

TO GRILL: Cover and grill lamb 5 to 6 inches from medium coals about 12 minutes, turning and brushing with orange mixture once, until desired doneness.

Ground Lamb Stroganoff

1 pound ground lamb
1 medium onion, chopped (about ½ cup)
1 can (10¾ ounces) condensed cream of
  chicken soup
1 can (4 ounces) mushroom stems and
  pieces, drained
½ teaspoon seasoned salt
¼ teaspoon pepper
½ cup sour cream or plain yogurt
Hot buttered spinach noodles
1 medium carrot, finely shredded

Cook and stir lamb and onion in 10-inch skillet until lamb is brown; drain. Stir in soup, mushrooms, seasoned salt and pepper. Heat to boiling; reduce heat. Simmer uncovered, stirring frequently, 5 minutes.

Stir in sour cream; heat just until hot. Serve over noodles; sprinkle with carrot.   **4 servings**

PER SERVING: Calories 490; Protein 25 g; Carbohydrate 32 g; Fat 29 g; Cholesterol 130 mg; Sodium 1,110 mg

GROUND BEEF STROGANOFF: Substitute 1 pound ground beef for the lamb.

MICROWAVE DIRECTIONS: Crumble ground lamb into 2-quart microwavable casserole; add onion. Cover with waxed paper and microwave on high 3 minutes; stir. Cover with waxed paper and microwave until no longer pink, 2 to 3 minutes longer; drain.

Stir in soup, mushrooms, seasoned salt and pepper. Cover tightly and microwave 3 minutes; stir. Cover tightly and microwave to boiling, 2 to 3 minutes longer. Stir in sour cream. Cover tightly and microwave until hot, 1 to 2 minutes. Serve over noodles; sprinkle with carrot.

Lamb with Yogurt-Mint Sauce

Lamb with Yogurt-Mint Sauce

This easy mint sauce is lovely with other lamb dishes, or vegetables.

²/₃ **cup plain nonfat yogurt**
¼ **cup firmly packed fresh mint leaves**
2 **tablespoons sugar**
4 **lamb loin chops, about 1 inch thick**
   (about 1 pound)

Place yogurt, mint and sugar in blender or food processor. Cover and blend or process until smooth.

Set oven control to broil. Spray broiler pan rack with nonstick cooking spray. Trim fat from lamb chops. Place lamb on rack in broiler pan. Broil with tops 2 to 3 inches from heat 12 to 14 minutes, turning lamb after 6 minutes, until desired doneness. Serve with sauce. **4 servings**

PER SERVING: Calories 255; Protein 34 g; Carbohydrate 9 g; Fat 9 g; Cholesterol 115 mg; Sodium 105 mg

Ground Lamb Kabobs

These spiced minced-meat kabobs are grilled on skewers, then tucked into pita bread for serving.

6 **pita breads, cut into halves**
1½ **pounds ground lamb**
1 **medium onion, chopped (about ½ cup)**
1 **cup snipped parsley leaves**
1¼ **teaspoons salt**
½ **teaspoon coarsely ground pepper**
½ **teaspoon ground cumin**
½ **teaspoon paprika**
¼ **teaspoon ground nutmeg**
Vegetable oil
2 **medium tomatoes, chopped**
4 **green onions (with tops), sliced**
Plain yogurt

Place lamb, onion, parsley, salt, pepper, cumin, paprika and nutmeg in food processor workbowl fitted with steel blade; cover and process with about 20 on/off motions until mixture forms a paste.

Divide lamb mixture into 12 equal parts. Shape each part into a roll, 5 × 1 inch. (For easy shaping, dip hands in cold water from time to time.) Place 2 rolls lengthwise on each of six 14-inch metal skewers. Brush kabobs with oil.

Grill kabobs about 4 inches from medium coals, turning 2 or 3 times, until no longer pink inside, 10 to 12 minutes. Remove kabobs from skewers; serve on pita bread halves topped with tomatoes, green onions and yogurt.

6 servings

PER SERVING: Calories 410; Protein 24 g; Carbohydrate 31 g; Fat 21 g; Cholesterol 75 mg; Sodium 730 mg

Pork Chops with Rhubarb Sauce

Red rhubarb gives the sauce a bold, pink color. Chop the rhubarb well; if the pieces are too large, the sauce will be stringy.

4 lean rib or loin pork chops, about ½ inch thick each
1 teaspoon dried rosemary leaves
½ teaspoon salt
¼ teaspoon pepper
2 cups chopped rhubarb (about 6 medium stalks)
¼ cup unsweetened apple juice
1 tablespoon packed brown sugar
1 tablespoon cornstarch
2 tablespoons cold water

Set oven control to broil. Trim fat from pork chops. Mix rosemary, salt and pepper; rub over pork. Place pork on rack sprayed with nonstick cooking spray in broiler pan. Broil pork with tops 3 to 5 inches from heat 10 minutes; turn pork. Broil until done, 5 to 10 minutes longer.

Heat rhubarb, apple juice and brown sugar to boiling; reduce heat. Cover and simmer until rhubarb is tender, about 10 minutes. Mix cornstarch and water; stir into rhubarb. Heat to boiling; boil and stir until thickened, about 1 minute. Serve with pork chops. **4 servings**

PER SERVING: Calories 285; Protein 17 g; Carbohydrate 10 g; Fat 19 g; Cholesterol 65 mg; Sodium 320 mg

MICROWAVE DIRECTIONS: Decrease apple juice to 3 tablespoons. Prepare pork chops as directed. Arrange pork, narrow ends toward center, in square microwavable dish, 8 × 8 × 2 inches. Cover with vented plastic wrap and microwave on medium (50%), rotating dish ¼ turn every 5 minutes until pork is done, 20 to 23 minutes. Let stand covered 5 minutes. Mix apple juice, brown sugar, cornstarch and water in 4-cup microwavable measure; stir in rhubarb. Cover and microwave on high, stirring every 2 minutes, until thickened, 4 to 6 minutes. Serve with pork chops.

Broiled Pork Chops and Onions

You can also grill zucchini or tomatoes to complete this tasty dish.

4 pork loin or rib chops, about ¾ inch thick each
2 medium onions
Salt to taste
Rubbed sage to taste
2 teaspoons margarine or butter, melted
Pepper to taste

Set oven control to broil. Place pork chops on rack in broiler pan. Broil with tops 3 to 5 inches from heat until light brown, about 10 minutes. Turn pork.

Cut ¼-inch slice from both ends of each onion. Cut onions crosswise into halves; place in broiler pan with pork. Sprinkle salt and sage over onions. Broil until onions are light brown, about 5 minutes; turn onions. Sprinkle with salt and sage; drizzle with margarine. Broil until pork is done, about 5 minutes longer. Sprinkle salt and pepper over pork. **4 servings**

PER SERVING: Calories 310; Protein 21 g; Carbohydrate 5 g; Fat 23 g; Cholesterol 70 mg; Sodium 130 mg

TO GRILL: Grill pork and onions 4 inches from medium coals, turning 1 or 2 times and brushing onions with margarine, until pork is done (170°), about 20 minutes. Sprinkle salt and sage over onions; sprinkle salt and pepper over pork.

Broiled Pork Chops and Onions

Gingered Pork with Peaches

1 pound pork tenderloin
1 tablespoon vegetable oil
2 tablespoons soy sauce
2 tablespoons finely chopped gingerroot
   or 1 teaspoon ground ginger
2 teaspoons cornstarch
1/8 teaspoon pepper
2 cloves garlic, finely chopped
2 tablespoons vegetable oil
1/2 cup slivered almonds
1/2 cup chicken broth
3 medium peaches, pared and sliced
6 green onions (with tops), cut into 1-
   inch pieces
3 cups hot cooked rice

Trim fat from pork tenderloin. Cut pork with grain into 2-inch strips. Cut strips across grain into 1/4-inch slices. (For ease in cutting, partially freeze pork about 1 1/2 hours.) Toss pork with 1 tablespoon oil, the soy sauce, gingerroot, cornstarch, pepper and garlic.

Heat 2 tablespoons oil in 10-inch skillet over medium-high heat until hot. Rotate skillet until oil covers bottom. Stir-fry pork and almonds 6 to 8 minutes or until pork is brown. Add chicken broth. Stir about 1 minute or until thickened. Add peaches and onions. Stir about 3 minutes or until peaches are hot. Serve over rice.

6 servings

PER SERVING: Calories 315; Protein 21 g; Carbohydrate 34 g; Fat 10 g; Cholesterol 50 mg; Sodium 830 mg

NOTE: 1 package (16 ounces) frozen sliced peaches, thawed and drained, can be substituted for the fresh peaches.

Sesame Pork with Garlic-Cream Sauce

Cream cheese is the key to this quick sauce.

1 1/2 pounds pork tenderloin
2 tablespoons vegetable oil
1/4 cup sesame seeds
1 tablespoon margarine or butter
2 cloves garlic, finely chopped
1 package (3 ounces) cream cheese, cut
   into cubes
1/3 cup milk
1 tablespoon chopped fresh or 1 teaspoon freeze-dried chives

Cut pork tenderloin crosswise into 12 slices. Flatten slices to 1/2-inch thickness. Set oven control to broil. Brush pork with oil. Place pork on rack in broiler pan. Sprinkle with half the sesame seeds. Broil pork with tops 3 to 5 inches from heat 6 minutes; turn. Sprinkle with remaining sesame seeds. Broil about 5 minutes or until pork is no longer pink in center.

Heat margarine in 10-inch skillet over medium heat. Cook garlic in margarine about 2 minutes, stirring occasionally; reduce heat. Add cream cheese and milk. Cook, stirring constantly, until smooth and hot. Stir in chives. Serve with pork.

6 servings

PER SERVING: Calories 240; Protein 19 g; Carbohydrate 2 g; Fat 17 g; Cholesterol 65 mg; Sodium 110 mg

TO GRILL: After brushing pork with oil, coat with sesame seeds. Cover and grill 5 to 6 inches from medium coals 12 to 15 minutes, turning once, until pork is no longer pink in center. Continue as directed.

Pork and Broccoli Risotto

The method below is a shortcut to a time-consuming traditional one, where broth is added very gradually. This risotto still achieves a slightly firm texture, just as it should. The grains of Arborio rice are shorter and fatter than those of ordinary rice.

1 pound lean pork boneless loin or leg
2 teaspoons vegetable oil
3 cups broccoli flowerets
1 cup chopped red bell pepper
2 cloves garlic, finely chopped
1 teaspoon salt
½ cup chopped onion (about 1 medium)
1 tablespoon reduced-calorie margarine
1 cup uncooked long-grain or Arborio rice
¼ cup dry white wine or chicken broth
1 cup beef broth
1¼ cups water
¼ cup skim mllk
2 tablespoons grated Parmesan cheese

Trim fat from pork loin; cut pork into slices, 2 × 1 × ¼ inch. Heat vegetable oil in 10-inch nonstick skillet over medium heat. Cook and stir pork, broccoli, bell pepper, garlic and salt in oil until pork is done and vegetables are crisp-tender, about 5 minutes. Remove from skillet; keep warm.

In same skillet, cook onion in margarine until onion is tender, about 3 minutes. Stir in rice and wine; cook and stir until wine is absorbed, about 30 seconds. Stir in broth and water; heat to boiling. Reduce heat; cover and cook until rice is almost tender and mixture is creamy, about 15 minutes. Stir in milk and reserved pork mixture; heat through. Sprinkle with Parmesan cheese. **6 servings**

PER SERVING: Calories 230; Protein 13 g; Carbohydrate 5 g; Fat 15 g; Cholesterol 45 mg; Sodium 650 mg

Picante Pork Chile

1 medium onion, chopped (about ½ cup)
1 medium green bell pepper, chopped (about 1 cup)
1 clove garlic, finely chopped
½ pound ground pork
1 cup salsa
1 teaspoon chile powder
¼ teaspoon salt
1 can (16 ounces) pinto beans, rinsed and drained
1 can (16 ounces) whole tomatoes, undrained

Cook onion, bell pepper, garlic and pork in 3-quart saucepan over medium heat, stirring frequently, until pork is no longer pink; drain if necessary. Stir in remaining ingredients, breaking up tomatoes. Cover and simmer 10 minutes. **4 servings**

PER SERVING: Calories 370; Protein 22 g; Carbohydrate 44 g; Fat 12 g; Cholesterol 35 mg; Sodium 1,240 mg

Ham and Zucchini with Poppy Seeds

1 medium onion, thinly sliced
2 tablespoons margarine or butter
3 cups cut-up fully cooked smoked ham
4 small zucchini (about 1 pound), cut into ¼-inch strips
1 green bell pepper, cut into ¼-inch slices
⅛ teaspoon pepper
½ cup sour cream
1 teaspoon poppy seeds

Cook and stir onion in margarine in 10-inch skillet until tender. Stir in ham, zucchini, bell pepper and pepper. Cover and cook over medium heat, stirring occasionally, until vegetables are crisp-tender, about 8 minutes.

Stir in sour cream and poppy seeds; heat just until hot. Serve with hot cooked rice or noodles if desired. **6 servings**

PER SERVING: Calories 260; Protein 16 g; Carbohydrate 6 g; Fat 19 g; Cholesterol 55 mg; Sodium 720 mg

Rolled Ham and Gruyère Omelet

An easy omelet that is baked instead of fried in a skillet.

½ cup all-purpose flour
1 cup milk
2 tablespoons margarine or butter, melted
½ teaspoon salt
4 eggs
1 cup coarsely chopped, fully cooked smoked ham
1 small onion, chopped (about ¼ cup)
1½ cups shredded Gruyère or Swiss cheese (6 ounces)
1 cup chopped fresh spinach

Heat oven to 350°. Line jelly roll pan, 15½ × 10½ x 1 inch, with aluminum foil. Generously grease foil. Beat flour, milk, margarine, salt and eggs until well blended; pour into pan. Sprinkle with ham and onion.

Bake until eggs are set, 15 to 18 minutes. Immediately sprinkle with cheese and spinach; roll up, beginning at narrow end and using foil to lift and roll omelet. Arrange additional spinach leaves on serving plate if desired. Cut omelet into 1½-inch slices. **6 servings**

PER SERVING: Calories 295; Protein 20 g; Carbohydrate 13 g; Fat 18 g; Cholesterol 185 mg; Sodium 720 mg

ROLLED BACON AND GRUYÈRE OMELET: Substitute 8 slices cooked bacon, crisp and crumbled, for the ham.

ROLLED SAUSAGE AND GRUYÈRE OMELET: Substitute 1 package (8 ounces) fully cooked sausage links, cut up, for the ham.

Rolled Ham and Gruyère Omelet

Soup Shortcuts

Putting together a quick soup can round out a meal very nicely—and deliciously.

• To make broth from bouillon: For each cup of broth, simply dissolve 1 bouillon cube or 1 teaspoon instant bouillon in 1 cup boiling water.

• Make an impromptu soup by adding leftover cooked vegetables to broth or bouillon. Add your favorite spices and some croutons or crackers for garnish, and you have a delicious soup in no time.

• Add leftover meats to canned or prepared dry soup mixes, then flavor with herbs.

• Blend or process 1 package (8 ounces) cream cheese, softened, and 1 chilled 16-ounce can fruit for an easy fruit soup. Stir in additional liquid, if necessary, until desired thickness. Add cinnamon, nutmeg or allspice to taste.

Vegetable and Ham Omelet

1 package (12 ounces) loose-pack frozen hash brown potatoes
¼ cup vegetable oil
1 package (4 ounces) sliced fully cooked smoked ham, cut into ½-inch strips
1 medium onion, chopped (about ½ cup)
6 eggs
½ teaspoon salt
⅛ teaspoon pepper
1 cup frozen whole kernel corn
2 tablespoons margarine or butter
Grated Parmesan cheese

Cook and stir potatoes in oil in 10-inch skillet over medium heat until tender, about 5 minutes. Stir in ham and onion. Cook, stirring occasionally, until onion is tender, about 5 minutes.

Beat eggs, salt and pepper. Stir corn and margarine into ham mixture; pour eggs over top. Cover and cook over medium-low heat until eggs are set and light brown on bottom, about 10 minutes. Sprinkle with cheese; cut into wedges.

6 servings

PER SERVING: Calories 400; Protein 15 g; Carbohydrate 20 g; Fat 29 g; Cholesterol 230 mg; Sodium 820 mg

NOTE: 1 can (8 ounces) whole kernel corn, drained, can be substituted for the 1 cup frozen corn.

2
Pleasing Poultry

Chicken Breasts in Mustard Sauce

Different types of mustard will make subtle and delicious changes in the flavor of this dish.

2 tablespoons margarine or butter
4 skinless boneless chicken breast
    halves (about 1 pound)
1 small onion, finely chopped (about
    ¼ cup)
2 tablespoons apple brandy or apple
    juice
1 cup whipping (heavy) cream
2 tablespoons snipped fresh parsley
2 tablespoons Dijon mustard
¼ cup finely chopped walnuts

Heat margarine in 10-inch skillet over medium heat. Add chicken breasts. Cook 12 to 14 minutes, turning after 6 minutes, until juices run clear. Remove chicken and reserve.

Add onion and brandy to skillet. Heat to boiling; reduce heat. Stir in whipping cream, parsley and mustard. Cook and stir over medium heat 5 minutes. Add chicken and walnuts. Heat until hot. **4 servings**

PER SERVING: Calories 395; Protein 19 g; Carbohydrate 5 g; Fat 34 g; Cholesterol 125 mg; Sodium 225 mg

Chicken Breasts in Lemon-Caper Sauce

4 skinless boneless chicken breast
    halves (about 1½ pounds)
½ cup all-purpose flour
¼ cup butter or margarine
2 teaspoons chopped garlic
1 cup dry white wine or chicken broth
2 tablespoons lemon juice
½ teaspoon pepper
1 tablespoon large capers, drained
Strawberries
Parsley sprigs

Cut each chicken breast horizontally to make 2 thin slices. Coat with flour. Heat butter in 12-inch skillet over medium-high heat. Cook chicken and garlic in butter 4 to 6 minutes, turning once, until chicken is brown. Add wine and lemon juice; sprinkle with pepper. Heat until hot. Sprinkle with capers. Garnish with strawberries and parsley. **4 servings**

PER SERVING: Calories 360; Protein 39 g; Carbohydrate 15 g; Fat 16 g; Cholesterol 125 mg; Sodium 170 mg

Oriental Barbecued Chicken

Oriental Barbecued Chicken

Chicken thighs can be substituted for the breasts here.

**4 skinless boneless chicken breast
halves (about 1 pound)**
½ cup hoisin sauce
1 tablespoon sesame oil
1 tablespoon no-salt-added tomato paste
½ teaspoon ground ginger
2 cloves garlic, crushed

Set oven control to broil. Trim fat from chicken breast halves. Place chicken on rack in broiler pan. Mix remaining ingredients; brush on chicken. Broil with tops about 4 inches from heat 7 to 8 minutes or until brown; turn. Brush with sauce. Broil 4 to 5 minutes longer or until juices of chicken run clear. Heat remaining sauce to boiling. Serve with chicken.   **4 servings**

PER SERVING: Calories 305; Protein 49 g; Carbohydrate 3 g; Fat 9 g; Cholesterol 135 mg; Sodium 170 mg

Lemon Chicken

2 tablespoons margarine or butter
**4 small skinless boneless chicken breast
halves (about 1 pound)**
½ cup dry white wine or chicken broth
1 tablespoon lemon juice
¼ teaspoon salt
1 lemon, thinly sliced
**2 tablespoons sliced green onions (with
tops)**

Heat margarine in 10-inch skillet until melted. Cook chicken in margarine over medium heat about 10 minutes or until brown on both sides. Add wine and lemon juice. Sprinkle with salt. Place lemon slices on chicken. Heat to boiling; reduce heat.

Cover and simmer 10 to 15 minutes or until chicken is done. Remove chicken; keep warm. Heat wine mixture to boiling. Cook 3 minutes or until reduced to about half. Pour over chicken. Sprinkle with green onions.   **4 servings**

PER SERVING: Calories 190; Protein 25 g; Carbohydrate 2 g; Fat 9 g; Cholesterol 60 mg; Sodium 260 mg

Chicken Almond

2 tablespoons vegetable oil
**1 large whole chicken breast (about 1
pound) skinned, boned and cut into ⅛-
inch strips**
1 can (8 ounces) bamboo shoots, drained
**1 large stalk celery, cut diagonally into
¼-inch slices (about ¾ cup)**
**8 ounces mushrooms, cut into ¼-inch
slices**
¼ teaspoon ground ginger
¾ cup chicken broth
2 teaspoons soy sauce
2 tablespoons cornstarch
3 tablespoons cold water
½ cup toasted whole blanched almonds
Hot cooked rice

Heat oil in 10-inch skillet until a few drops of water sprinkled in skillet skitter around. Add chicken. Cook and stir over medium-high heat until almost done, about 6 minutes. Add bamboo shoots, celery, mushrooms and ginger. Cook and stir 1 minute. Stir in broth and soy sauce; reduce heat. Cover and simmer until vegetables are crisp-tender and chicken is done, 3 to 5 minutes.

Shake cornstarch and cold water in tightly covered container; stir gradually into chicken mixture. Heat to boiling, stirring constantly. Boil and stir 1 minute. Top with almonds and serve with hot rice.   **4 servings**

PER SERVING: Calories 485; Protein 34 g; Carbohydrate 42 g; Fat 20 g; Cholesterol 60 mg; Sodium 790 mg

Spicy Chicken with Broccoli

If you can't find brown bean sauce, substitute the same amount of dark soy sauce.

2 whole chicken breasts (about
   2 pounds)
2 teaspoons cornstarch
½ teaspoon salt
¼ teaspoon white pepper
1 pound broccoli
3 green onions with tops
1 jalapeño chile or 1 teaspoon dried red
   pepper flakes
3 tablespoons vegetable oil
2 tablespoons brown bean sauce
2 teaspoons finely chopped garlic
1 teaspoon sugar
1 teaspoon finely chopped gingerroot

Remove skin and bones from chicken breasts; cut chicken into 2 × ½-inch pieces. Toss chicken, cornstarch, salt and white pepper in medium bowl. Cover and refrigerate 20 minutes.

Pare outer layer from broccoli. Cut broccoli lengthwise into 1-inch stems; remove flowerets. Cut stems diagonally into ¼-inch slices. Place broccoli flowerets and stems in boiling water; heat to boiling. Cover and cook 1 minute; drain. Immediately rinse with cold water; drain. Cut onions diagonally into 1-inch pieces. Remove seeds and membrane from chile. Cut chile into very thin slices.

Heat wok or 12-inch skillet until very hot. Add oil; rotate wok to coat side. Add chile, bean sauce, garlic, sugar and gingerroot; stir-fry 10 seconds. Add chicken; stir-fry 2 minutes or until chicken is white. Add broccoli and onions; stir-fry 1 minute or until broccoli is hot.

4 servings

PER SERVING: Calories 305; Protein 37 g; Carbohydrate 10 g; Fat 13 g; Cholesterol 85 mg; Sodium 420 mg

Chicken–Chutney Stir-Fry

1 tablespoon vegetable oil
3 skinless boneless chicken breast halves
   (about 1 pound), cut into 1-inch pieces
2 carrots, thinly sliced (about 1 cup)
½ medium red bell pepper, cut into thin
   strips
1 tablespoon cornstarch
1 tablespoon soy sauce
½ cup chutney
6 ounces pea pods
¼ cup chopped peanuts

Heat oil in 10-inch skillet or wok until hot. Add chicken, carrots and bell pepper. Stir-fry over medium-high heat 5 to 7 minutes or until chicken is white. Mix cornstarch, soy sauce and chutney. Stir into chicken mixture. Cook and stir over medium heat until slightly thickened. Stir in pea pods; heat until hot. Serve over rice. Sprinkle with peanuts.

4 servings

PER SERVING: Calories 300; Protein 29 g; Carbohydrate 21 g; Fat 11 g; Cholesterol 60 mg; Sodium 380 mg

Quick Changes for Pasta and Rice

Stir one of the following into cooked pasta or rice for a flavorful side dish.

Fresh or dried herbs
Leftover vegetables
Crisply cooked bacon or fully cooked
   smoked ham
Water chestnuts and soy sauce
Raisins, citrus peel and juice
Chopped onion, celery and garlic
Chutney and peanuts
Salsa
Barbecue sauce
Pimiento and olives
Chopped green chiles
Shredded cheese

Chicken–Chutney Stir-Fry

Peanutty Chicken Kabobs

The unusual sauce for these kabobs comes from an old standby—the crunchy peanut butter in your cupboard.

1 pound skinless boneless chicken breast halves or thighs
⅓ cup crunchy peanut butter
⅓ cup boiling water
1 tablespoon grated gingerroot or 1 teaspoon ground ginger
1 tablespoon lemon juice
⅛ teaspoon crushed red pepper

Cut chicken into 1½-inch pieces. Mix remaining ingredients. Reserve ¼ cup. Set oven control to broil. Thread chicken cubes on four 11-inch metal skewers, leaving space between each. Brush chicken with half of the reserved peanut butter mixture.

Broil chicken with tops about 4 inches from heat about 5 minutes or until brown. Turn and brush with remaining reserved peanut butter mixture. Broil 5 minutes or until golden brown. Serve with peanut butter mixture and chopped peanuts if desired. **4 servings**

PER KABOB: Calories 215; Protein 21 g; Carbohydrate 5 g; Fat 12 g; Cholesterol 45 mg; Sodium 140 mg

TO GRILL: Cover and grill kabobs 4 to 5 inches from medium coals 15 to 25 minutes, turning and brushing with peanut butter mixture, until golden brown.

Open-Face Pita Sandwiches

½ jar (8-ounce size) sun-dried tomatoes in oil, drained, and 2 tablespoons oil reserved
4 small skinless boneless chicken breast halves (about 1 pound), cut into about ½-inch pieces
¼ teaspoon Italian seasoning
1 small onion, thinly sliced
¼ cup grated Parmesan cheese
2 whole wheat pita breads (6 inches in diameter)
½ cup shredded mozzarella cheese (2 ounces)

Heat oven to 375°. Heat reserved oil in 10-inch skillet over medium-high heat until hot. Sauté chicken, Italian seasoning and onion in oil about 4 minutes, stirring frequently, until chicken turns white. Cut tomatoes into ¼-inch strips. Stir tomatoes and Parmesan cheese into chicken mixture.

Split each pita bread in half around edge with knife to make 4 rounds. Divide chicken mixture evenly among rounds. Sprinkle with mozzarella cheese. Bake about 5 minutes or until cheese is melted. **4 servings**

PER SERVING: Calories 325; Protein 35 g; Carbohydrate 26 g; Fat 9 g; Cholesterol 75 mg; Sodium 520 mg

Open-Face Pita Sandwiches

Waldorf Chicken

This is an unusual variation on the popular salad that turns chicken into a masterpiece.

6 small chicken breast halves (about 3 pounds), skinned and boned
1 cup unsweetened apple juice
1 tablespoon lemon juice
¼ teaspoon salt
¼ teaspoon ground ginger
1 tablespoon cornstarch
2 cups coarsely chopped unpared red apples (about 2 medium)
1 cup diagonally cut celery slices (about 2 medium stalks)
3 tablespoons raisins
1 tablespoon sliced green onion (with top)

Remove fat from chicken. Place chicken, ½ cup of the apple juice, the lemon juice, salt and ginger in 10-inch nonstick skillet. Heat to boiling; reduce heat. Cover and simmer until done, about 20 minutes. Remove chicken; keep warm.

Mix remaining apple juice and the cornstarch; add to hot liquid. Heat to boiling, stirring constantly. Boil and stir 1 minute. Stir in remaining ingredients; heat through. For each serving, diagonally slice chicken breast, overlapping slices. Top with sauce. **6 servings**

PER SERVING: Calories 240; Protein 33 g; Carbohydrate 18 g; Fat 4 g; Cholesterol 85 mg; Sodium 180 mg

MICROWAVE DIRECTIONS: Decrease apple juice to ¾ cup. Place chicken, ½ cup of the apple juice, the lemon juice, salt and ginger in 3-quart microwavable casserole. Cover tightly and microwave on high 6 minutes; rotate casserole ½ turn. Microwave until chicken is done, 6 to 8 minutes longer. Remove chicken; keep warm. Mix remaining apple juice and the cornstarch; add to hot liquid. Microwave uncovered, stirring every minute until thickened, 3 to 4 minutes. Stir in remaining ingredients and microwave until hot, 2 to 3 minutes. Continue as directed.

Curried Chicken And Nectarines

4 skinless boneless chicken breast halves (about 1 pound)
2 tablespoons reduced-calorie oil-and-vinegar dressing
1 teaspoon curry powder
¼ cup raisins
¼ cup sliced green onions (with tops)
¼ teaspoon salt
1 medium bell pepper, cut into ¼-inch strips
2 small nectarines, cut into ¼-inch slices

Trim fat from chicken breast halves. Cut chicken crosswise into ½-inch strips. Mix dressing and curry powder in medium bowl. Add chicken; toss. Heat 10-inch nonstick skillet over medium-high heat. Stir in chicken and remaining ingredients except nectarines; stir-fry 4 to 6 minutes or until chicken is done. Stir in nectarines carefully; heat through. Serve with hot cooked rice or couscous if desired. **4 servings**

PER SERVING: Calories 210; Protein 25 g; Carbohydrate 15 g; Fat 6 g; Cholesterol 80 mg; Sodium 230 mg

MICROWAVE DIRECTIONS: Prepare chicken as directed. Mix dressing and curry powder in 2-quart microwavable casserole. Add chicken; toss. Stir in remaining ingredients except nectarines. Cover tightly and microwave on high 8 to 10 minutes, stirring after 4 minutes, until chicken is done. Stir in nectarines carefully. Cover and microwave 1 minute or until heated through.

Easy Chicken Curry

2 tablespoons margarine or butter
1 teaspoon curry powder
1 small onion, chopped (about ¼ cup)
2 cups cut-up cooked chicken or turkey
⅓ cup raisins
1 small unpared all-purpose red apple,
  coarsely chopped
1 can (10¾ ounces) condensed cream of
  chicken soup
1 soup can water
Hot cooked rice
Chopped peanuts

Cook and stir margarine, curry powder and onion in 3-quart saucepan over medium heat until onion is tender, about 4 minutes.

Stir in remaining ingredients except rice and peanuts. Cook, stirring occasionally, until hot. Serve over rice; sprinkle with peanuts and, if desired, additional raisins. **4 servings**

PER SERVING: Calories 610; Protein 49 g; Carbohydrate 52 g; Fat 23 g; Cholesterol 120 mg; Sodium 1,210 mg

NOTE: Stir hot cooked green peas into rice before serving if desired.

Curried Chicken Thighs

4 skinless boneless chicken thighs
  (about 1 pound)
1 tablespoon vegetable oil
1 teaspoon curry powder
½ teaspoon salt
Dash of ground ginger
Dash of ground cumin
1 small onion, chopped (about ¼ cup)
⅓ cup water
½ cup sour cream

Cut chicken thighs into 1-inch strips. Heat oil in 10-inch skillet until hot. Cook chicken in oil over medium-high heat until brown on all sides. Sprinkle with remaining ingredients except sour cream; reduce heat. Cover and simmer about 10 minutes or until chicken is done. Stir in sour cream. **4 servings**

PER SERVING: Calories 250; Protein 25 g; Carbohydrate 2 g; Fat 16 g; Cholesterol 95 mg; Sodium 350 mg

Raspberry–Chicken Salad

Try fresh black and golden raspberries for an interesting alternative.

4 cups bite-size pieces mixed salad
  greens (iceberg, Bibb, romaine or
  spinach)
2 cups cut-up cooked chicken
1 cup raspberries
⅓ cup thinly sliced celery
¼ cup toasted sliced almonds
Raspberry Dressing (below)
Freshly ground pepper

Toss salad greens, chicken, raspberries and celery; sprinkle with almonds. Serve with Raspberry Dressing and pepper. **4 servings**

PER SERVING: Calories 250; Protein 26 g; Carbohydrate 12 g; Fat 11 g; Cholesterol 60 mg; Sodium 130 mg

Raspberry Dressing

1 cup nonfat plain yogurt
½ cup raspberries
1 tablespoon raspberry or red wine
  vinegar
2 teaspoons sugar

Place all ingredients in blender container. Cover and blend on high speed until smooth, about 15 seconds.

NOTE: Frozen, unsweetened, loose-pack raspberries can be substituted for the fresh raspberries.

Tarragon and Chicken Pasta

Tarragon with its distinctive aniselike flavor is a marvelous seasoning for chicken, fish and vegetables.

1 cup uncooked spiral pasta (about 4 ounces)
2 cups sliced mushrooms (about 5 ounces)
1 cup broccoli flowerets
1 cup thinly sliced carrots (about 2 large)
1 cup skim milk
1 tablespoon cornstarch
2 teaspoons chopped fresh or ½ teaspoon dried tarragon leaves
¼ teaspoon salt
1 clove garlic, finely chopped
2 cups shredded spinach or romaine lettuce (about 3 ounces)
1½ cups cut-up cooked chicken or turkey (about 8 ounces)
½ cup shredded Swiss cheese (2 ounces)

Cook pasta as directed on package—except add mushrooms, broccoli and carrots during last 4 minutes of cooking; drain.

Mix milk, cornstarch, tarragon, salt and garlic in 1½-quart saucepan. Cook over medium heat 4 minutes, stirring constantly, until mixture thickens and boils. Stir in remaining ingredients until cheese is melted and spinach is wilted. Toss with pasta mixture. **4 servings**

PER SERVING: Calories 315; Protein 27 g; Carbohydrate 35 g; Fat 7 g; Cholesterol 55 mg; Sodium 280 mg

Pasta Shells with Chicken and Broccoli

For variety, try different shapes and flavors of pasta. Use similar-size pastas, so cooking time is consistent.

6 ounces uncooked pasta shells or wheels
1 cup chopped broccoli
⅓ cup chopped onion (about 1 medium)
2 cloves garlic, finely chopped
1 carrot, cut into very thin strips
2 tablespoons vegetable oil
2 cups cut-up cooked chicken or turkey
1 teaspoon salt
2 large tomatoes, chopped (about 2 cups)
⅓ cup grated Parmesan cheese
2 tablespoons chopped fresh parsley

Cook pasta as directed on package; drain. Cook broccoli, onion, garlic and carrot in oil in 10-inch skillet over medium heat about 10 minutes, stirring occasionally, until broccoli is crisp-tender.

Stir in chicken, salt and tomatoes. Cook uncovered about 3 minutes or just until chicken is hot. Spoon over pasta. Sprinkle with cheese and parsley. **6 servings**

PER SERVING: Calories 325; Protein 20 g; Carbohydrate 33 g; Fat 12 g; Cholesterol 40 mg; Sodium 490 mg

Oriental Chicken Salad

Cellophane noodles are hard, clear noodles made from mung peas. They become white, puffy and crisp when deep-fried, puffing up to more than twice their original size. Remove them quickly from the oil so they stay white.

Ginger Dressing (right)
Vegetable oil
1 package (3¾ ounces) cellophane noodles (bean threads)
½ head lettuce, shredded (about 4 cups)
3 cups cut-up cooked chicken or turkey
1 medium carrot, shredded (about ½ cup)
4 green onions (with tops) sliced (about ¼ cup)
1 tablespoon sesame seeds, toasted

Prepare Ginger Dressing. Heat oil (1 inch) in Dutch oven to 425°. Fry one-quarter of the noodles at a time about 5 seconds, turning once, until puffed; drain.

Pour Ginger Dressing over lettuce, chicken, carrot and onions in large bowl. Toss with half of the noodles. Place remaining noodles on large platter. Spoon salad over noodles. Sprinkle with sesame seeds.   **6 servings**

PER SERVING: Calories 490; Protein 25 g; Carbohydrate 28 g; Fat 31 g; Cholesterol 65 mg; Sodium 650 mg

---

NOTE: 5 cups chow mein noodles can be substituted for the fried cellophane noodles. Toss half of the noodles with chicken-dressing mixture. Continue as directed.

Ginger Dressing

⅓ cup vegetable oil
¼ cup white wine vinegar
1 tablespoon sugar
2 teaspoons soy sauce
½ teaspoon pepper
½ teaspoon ground ginger
¼ teaspoon salt

Shake all ingredients in tightly covered container. Refrigerate at least 2 hours.

Pasta Cooking Timetable

A handy guide for timing pasta.

Dried Packaged Pasta

Pasta	Cooking Time
Alphabets	4 to 5 minutes
Ditalini	8 to 9 minutes
Elbow Macaroni	8 to 10 minutes
Farfalle	11 to 12 minutes
Fettuccine	10 to 12 minutes
Lasagne	10 to 12 minutes
Linguine	8 to 10 minutes
Manicotti	10 to 12 minutes
Mostaccioli	12 to 14 minutes
Noodles	6 to 8 minutes
Orzo or Rosamarina	5 to 8 minutes
Rigatoni	14 to 16 minutes
Rotini	10 to 12 minutes
Shell Macaroni, small	6 to 8 minutes
medium	10 to 12 minutes
jumbo	12 to 15 minutes
Spaghetti	8 to 10 minutes
Tortellini	25 to 30 minutes
Vermicelli	4 to 6 minutes
Ziti	12 to 14 minutes

Mexican Chicken Salad

Add extra crunch to this recipe by stirring in partially crushed tortilla chips just before serving.

2 cups cut-up cooked chicken
¼ cup sour cream
¼ cup mayonnaise or salad dressing
¼ cup finely chopped carrot
2 tablespoons chopped fresh cilantro leaves
2 tablespoons capers
2 tablespoons chopped pimiento
2 tablespoons lime juice
1½ teaspoons chopped fresh or ½ teaspoon dried oregano leaves
½ teaspoon ground cumin
1 small onion, chopped (about ¼ cup)
Lettuce leaves
1 avocado, peeled and cut into wedges
Paprika

Toss all ingredients except lettuce, avocado and paprika. Serve on lettuce with avocado. Sprinkle with paprika.   **4 servings**

PER SERVING: Calories 360; Protein 21 g; Carbohydrate 9 g; Fat 28 g; Cholesterol 65 mg; Sodium 150 mg

Glazed Turkey Tenderloins

2 turkey breast tenderloins (about 1¼ pounds)
1 tablespoon vegetable oil
⅓ cup orange marmalade
1 teaspoon finely chopped gingerroot or ½ teaspoon ground ginger
1 teaspoon Worcestershire sauce

Cook turkey breast tenderloins in oil in 10-inch skillet over medium heat about 5 minutes or until brown on one side; turn turkey. Stir in remaining ingredients; reduce heat.

Cover and simmer 15 to 20 minutes, stirring occasionally, until turkey is done and sauce is thickened. Cut turkey into thin slices. Spoon sauce over turkey.   **4 servings**

PER SERVING: Calories 280; Protein 33 g; Carbohydrate 19 g; Fat 8 g; Cholesterol 85 mg; Sodium 90 mg

Turkey Slices with Walnuts

2 tablespoons margarine or butter
1 package (about 16 ounces) uncooked turkey breast slices
¼ teaspoon salt
1 tablespoon margarine or butter
⅓ cup walnut pieces
2 green onions (with tops), sliced
1 teaspoon cornstarch
½ cup dry white wine or chicken broth
1 teaspoon sugar

Heat 2 tablespoons margarine in 12-inch skillet over medium-high heat until melted. Sauté turkey slices about 4 minutes or until brown on both sides, sprinkling with salt after turning. Remove from skillet; keep warm. Add 1 tablespoon margarine to skillet. Cook walnuts and green onions in margarine over medium heat 2 to 3 minutes or until onions are soft. Stir cornstarch into wine; pour into skillet. Add sugar. Heat to boiling; boil and stir 1 minute. Pour over turkey slices.

                   4 servings

PER SERVING: Calories 280; Protein 28 g; Carbohydrate 4 g; Fat 17 g; Cholesterol 65 mg; Sodium 300 mg

Glazed Turkey Tenderloins

Turkey Divan

Cooked turkey breast is easy to find in many supermarkets and most delis.

¼ **cup margarine or butter**
¼ **cup all-purpose flour**
⅛ **teaspoon ground nutmeg**
1½ **cups chicken broth**
½ **cup grated Parmesan cheese**
2 **tablespoons dry white wine or chicken broth**
½ **cup whipping (heavy) cream**
1½ **pounds broccoli or 2 packages (10 ounces each) frozen broccoli spears, cooked and drained**
6 **large slices cooked turkey breast (about ¾ pound)**
½ **cup grated Parmesan cheese**

Heat margarine in 1-quart saucepan over medium heat until melted. Stir in flour and nutmeg. Cook, stirring constantly, until smooth and bubbly; remove from heat. Stir in broth. Heat to boiling, stirring constantly. Boil and stir 1 minute; remove from heat. Stir in ½ cup cheese and the wine. Beat whipping cream in chilled bowl until stiff. Fold cheese mixture into whipped cream.

Place hot broccoli in ungreased rectangular baking dish, 12 × 7½ × 2 inches. Top with turkey. Pour cheese sauce over turkey. Sprinkle with ½ cup cheese. Set oven control to broil. Broil with top 3 to 5 inches from heat until cheese is bubbly and light brown.

6 servings

PER SERVING: Calories 370; Protein 28 g; Carbohydrate 12 g; Fat 23 g; Cholesterol 80 mg; Sodium 590 mg

Turkey Oven Sandwich

1 **pound ground turkey**
1 **tablespoon margarine or butter**
½ **teaspoon poultry seasoning**
2 **pita breads (6 inches in diameter), cut into halves**
1 **medium tomato, thinly sliced**
1 **stalk celery, sliced**
½ **cup shredded sharp Cheddar cheese (2 ounces)**
½ **cup sour cream**
⅓ **cup mayonnaise or salad dressing**
1 **tablespoon chopped onion**
Paprika, if desired

Heat oven to 425°. Cook and stir ground turkey, margarine and poultry seasoning in 10-inch skillet over medium heat until turkey is done; drain. Place pita breads on bottom and about halfway up sides of ungreased square pan, 9 × 9 × 2 inches (they will overlap slightly in middle). Layer turkey, tomato and celery on pitas. Mix remaining ingredients except paprika; spoon over top. Sprinkle with paprika. Bake 12 to 15 minutes or until topping is light brown.

4 servings

PER SERVING: Calories 595; Protein 32 g; Carbohydrate 27 g; Fat 40 g; Cholesterol 120 g; Sodium 520 mg

Turkey Oven Sandwich

Italian-style Turkey Patties

1 pound ground turkey
¼ cup dry bread crumbs
1 tablespoon lemon juice
1 tablespoon olive oil
1 teaspoon salt
1 teaspoon rubbed sage
¼ teaspoon pepper
3 slices provolone cheese or about 6 tablespoons shredded mozzarella cheese
1 tablespoon margarine or butter
6 cups shredded cabbage
Salt and pepper to taste

Mix ground turkey, bread crumbs, lemon juice, oil, salt, sage and pepper. Shape mixture into 6 thin patties, each about 5 inches in diameter. Cut each slice cheese into halves. Place half slice cheese on half of each patty; fold patty over cheese. Carefully press edge to seal.

Heat margarine in 12-inch skillet over medium heat until melted and bubbly. Cook patties in margarine until done, about 4 minutes on each side. Remove patties from skillet; keep warm.

Cook and stir cabbage in drippings in skillet until wilted, about 5 minutes. Sprinkle with salt and pepper. Serve with turkey patties; garnish with lemon wedges if desired.   **6 servings**

PER SERVING: Calories 250; Protein 20 g; Carbohydrate 7 g; Fat 16 g; Cholesterol 65 mg; Sodium 640 mg

Southwest Turkey Fajitas

To make this dish even more quickly, microwave the tortillas on high for 2 to 3 minutes; cover a microwavable dish with a damp microwavable paper towel instead of aluminum foil.

1 tablespoon lime juice
¼ teaspoon crushed red pepper
1 clove garlic, crushed
12 ounces cooked turkey, cut into about 2-inch strips (about 2 cups)
8 flour tortillas (7 inches in diameter)
1 tablespoon vegetable oil
1 container (6 ounces) frozen guacamole, thawed
1 jar (10 to 12 ounces) chunky red salsa

Heat oven to 325°. Mix lime juice, red pepper and garlic in glass or plastic bowl. Stir in turkey until well coated. Cover and refrigerate.

Wrap tortillas in aluminum foil; heat in oven about 15 minutes or until warm.

Heat oil in wok or 10-inch skillet over medium-high heat. Sauté turkey in oil about 2 minutes, stirring frequently, until turkey is hot.

Divide the turkey and guacamole among the tortillas. Top each with 2 tablespoons salsa. Fold 1 end of tortillas up about 1 inch over turkey mixture; fold right and left sides over folded ends, overlapping. Fold down remaining ends. Serve with remaining salsa.   **4 servings**

PER SERVING: Calories 495; Protein 32 g; Carbohydrate 51 g; Fat 18 g; Cholesterol 75 mg; Sodium 1,280 mg

Turkey–Pasta Primavera

6 ounces uncooked spaghetti or
   fettuccine
1 cup chopped broccoli
⅓ cup chopped onion (about 1 medium)
2 cloves garlic, finely chopped
½ cup julienne strips carrot (about
   1 medium)
1 tablespoon vegetable oil
2 cups cut-up cooked turkey or chicken
1 teaspoon salt
2 cups chopped tomatoes (about 2 large)
⅓ cup freshly grated Parmesan cheese
2 tablespoons chopped fresh parsley

Cook spaghetti as directed on package; drain.

Cook broccoli, onion, garlic and carrot in oil in 10-inch nonstick skillet over medium heat about 10 minutes, stirring occasionally, until broccoli is crisp-tender.

Stir in turkey, salt and tomatoes. Heat about 3 minutes or just until turkey is hot. Spoon over spaghetti. Sprinkle with cheese and parsley. **6 servings**

PER SERVING: Calories 300; Protein 21 g; Carbohydrate 34 g; Fat 9 g; Cholesterol 75 mg; Sodium 670 mg

Turkey–Pasta Salad

Spinach Sauce (below)
2 packages (5 ounces each) spiral
   pasta
3 cups cut-up cooked turkey or chicken
½ cup sliced ripe olives
1 tablespoon olive or vegetable oil
1 teaspoon vinegar
1 tablespoon pine nuts or slivered
   almonds

Prepare Spinach Sauce. Cook pasta as directed on package; drain. Rinse in cold water; drain. Toss macaroni and ½ cup of the Spinach Sauce. Mix turkey, olives, oil and vinegar. Spoon onto center of macaroni mixture. Sprinkle with pine nuts. Serve with remaining Spinach Sauce.

6 servings

PER SERVING: Calories 480; Protein 29 g; Carbohydrate 40 g; Fat 22 g; Cholesterol 65 mg; Sodium 300 mg

Spinach Sauce

4 cups spinach leaves
1 cup fresh parsley sprigs
¼ cup lemon juice
3 large cloves garlic, cut into halves
½ cup grated Parmesan cheese
2 tablespoons olive or vegetable oil
1 tablespoon chopped fresh or 1 teaspoon dried basil leaves
½ teaspoon pepper

Place half each of the spinach, parsley, lemon juice and garlic in blender or food processor. Cover and blend on medium speed about 3 minutes (stopping blender frequently to scrape sides) or process until spinach is finely chopped. Add remaining spinach, parsley, lemon juice and garlic; repeat. Add remaining ingredients. Cover and blend on medium speed about 2 minutes (stopping blender frequently to scrape sides) or process until mixture is smooth.

Cornmeal-fried Catfish

3

Speedy Fish and Seafood

═══════════════ ▣ ═══════════════

Oven-fried Fish

So easy—no basting, no turning, no constant watching!

1 pound lean fish fillets
¼ cup cornmeal
¼ cup dry bread crumbs
½ teaspoon paprika
¼ teaspoon salt
¾ teaspoon chopped fresh or ¼ teaspoon dried dill weed
⅛ teaspoon pepper
¼ cup milk
3 tablespoons margarine or butter, melted

Move oven rack to position slightly above middle of oven. Heat oven to 500°. Cut fish fillets into 2 × 1½-inch pieces. Mix cornmeal, bread crumbs, paprika, salt, dill weed and pepper. Dip fish into milk, then coat with cornmeal mixture.

Place fish in rectangular pan, 13 × 9 × 2 inches. Drizzle margarine over fish. Bake uncovered about 10 minutes or until fish flakes easily with fork. **4 servings**

PER SERVING: Calories 205; Protein 21 g; Carbohydrate 7 g; Fat 10 g; Cholesterol 35 mg; Sodium 305 mg

Cornmeal-fried Catfish

Try serving with corn bread and coleslaw for an authentic southern meal.

Vegetable oil
4 catfish fillets (about 4 ounces each)
¾ cup cornmeal
¼ cup all-purpose flour
¼ teaspoon salt
½ cup milk
2 eggs, beaten
⅛ teaspoon red pepper sauce
2 tablespoons vegetable oil

Heat oil (2 to 3 inches) in Dutch oven to 375°. Rinse catfish fillets and pat dry. Refrigerate until ready to use.

Mix cornmeal, flour and salt in large bowl. Stir in milk, eggs, pepper sauce and 2 tablespoons vegetable oil until well blended.

Coat fish with cornmeal batter, shaking off any excess. Fry fish in batches, 5 to 8 minutes or until golden brown. Drain on paper towels. Keep warm in 275° oven. **4 servings**

PER SERVING: Calories 490; Protein 31 g; Carbohydrate 28 g; Fat 28 g; Cholesterol 175 mg; Sodium 210 mg

Spicy Breaded Red Snapper

1 pound red snapper or other lean fish
  fillets
1½ cups seasoned croutons, crushed
1 teaspoon dry mustard
½ teaspoon salt
¼ teaspoon ground red pepper (cayenne)
⅛ teaspoon pepper
1 egg
1 tablespoon water
3 tablespoons margarine or butter,
  melted

Move oven rack to position slightly above middle of oven. Heat oven to 500°. Grease rectangular pan, 13 × 9 × 2 inches. If fillets are large, cut into 4 pieces. Mix croutons, mustard, salt, red pepper and pepper. Beat egg and water until well blended. Dip fish into egg, then coat with crouton mixture.

Place fish in pan. Drizzle margarine over fish. Bake uncovered about 10 minutes or until fish flakes easily with fork.   **4 servings**

PER SERVING: Calories 240; Protein 23 g; Carbohydrate 11 g; Fat 11 g; Cholesterol 100 mg; Sodium 595 mg

Quick Coatings

Try these quick coatings for whole fish or fillets when frying or baking:

Seasoned bread crumbs
Bread crumbs and Parmesan cheese
Bread crumbs and seasoning mix
Bread crumbs and dry salad dressing mix
Cornmeal and chile powder (or Cajun spice)
Crushed cornflakes or other cereal
Crushed corn chips

TO GRILL: Grease wire grill. Place fish fillets on grill. Grill 3 to 4 inches from medium coals 10 to 12 minutes, turning fish once and brushing with margarine, until fish flakes easily with fork.

Fish Fillets with Green Peppers and Mushrooms

Serve with hot cooked rice or Oriental noodles, if you like.

1 pound fish fillets
3 tablespoons soy sauce
¼ teaspoon ground ginger
1 clove garlic, finely chopped
2 medium green bell peppers, cut into
  1-inch pieces
8 ounces mushrooms, cut into halves
3 tablespoons vegetable oil

If fish fillets are large, cut into 4 serving pieces. Mix soy sauce, ginger and garlic; brush on both sides of fish. Cook and stir bell peppers and mushrooms in oil in 10-inch skillet over medium-high heat until crisp-tender, about 6 minutes. Remove vegetables with slotted spoon; reserve.

Cook fish in same skillet until fish flakes easily with fork, about 8 minutes. Add vegetables; heat just until hot.   **4 servings**

PER SERVING: Calories 230; Protein 24 g; Carbohydrate 7 g; Fat 12 g; Cholesterol 60 mg; Sodium 870 mg

MICROWAVE DIRECTIONS: Omit oil. Cut fish fillets into 4 serving pieces. Mix soy sauce, ginger and garlic; brush on both sides of fish. Arrange fish, with thickest parts to outside edges, in square microwavable dish, 8 × 8 × 2 inches. Top with vegetables. Cover with vented plastic wrap and microwave on high 4 minutes; rotate dish ½ turn. Microwave until fish flakes easily with fork and vegetables are crisp-tender, 4 to 5 minutes longer.

Salsa Fish

Cilantro, a southwestern favorite, is also known as fresh coriander, Mexican parsley and Chinese parsley. While cilantro resembles flat-leaf parsley, its flavor is more intense.

1 pound cod, orange roughy or other medium-fat fish fillets (about ½ inch thick)

1 cup chopped tomato (about 1 large)

½ cup chopped green bell pepper (about 1 small)

¼ cup chopped onion (about 1 small)

2 tablespoons finely chopped fresh cilantro or parsley

¼ teaspoon salt

¼ cup dry white wine or chicken broth

If fish fillets are large, cut into 4 serving pieces. Spray 10-inch nonstick skillet with nonstick cooking spray. Heat over medium heat. Arrange fish in single layer in skillet. Cook uncovered 4 to 6 minutes, turning once, until fish flakes easily with fork. Remove fish to warm platter; keep warm.

Cook remaining ingredients except wine in skillet over medium heat 3 to 5 minutes, stirring frequently, until bell pepper and onion are crisp-tender. Stir in wine. Heat until hot. Spoon tomato mixture over fish. **4 servings**

PER SERVING: Calories 150; Protein 24 g; Carbohydrate 6 g; Fat 2 g; Cholesterol 40 mg; Sodium 210 mg

Oriental Fish with Bok Choy

Bok Choy, also known as Chinese chard, is a favorite in Asian cuisines. It resembles a cross between chard and cabbage.

1 pound orange roughy or other lean fish fillets

½ pound bok choy

1 tablespoon sesame seeds

1 tablespoon vegetable oil

1 bunch green onions (with tops), cut into 2-inch pieces

1 small red bell pepper, cut into 1-inch pieces

½ cup chicken broth

½ teaspoon red pepper flakes

1 tablespoon cornstarch

1 tablespoon teriyaki sauce

2 cups hot cooked rice

Cut fish fillets into 1-inch pieces. Remove leaves from bok choy. Cut leaves into ½-inch strips and stems into ¼-inch slices. Cook sesame seeds in oil in 10-inch skillet over medium heat, stirring occasionally, until golden brown. Add bok choy stems, onions, bell pepper, fish, broth and pepper flakes. Heat to boiling; reduce heat. Cover and simmer about 5 minutes or until fish flakes easily with fork.

Mix cornstarch and teriyaki sauce. Gradually stir into fish mixture. Heat to boiling, stirring constantly. Boil and stir 1 minute. Stir in bok choy leaves and heat until wilted. Serve over rice. **4 servings**

PER SERVING: Calories 280; Protein 24 g; Carbohydrate 31 g; Fat 7 g; Cholesterol 30 mg; Sodium 650 mg

Mahimahi in Fennel Sauce

Mahimahi is the Hawaiian name for dolphinfish, which is not related to the mammal dolphin.

1½ pounds mahimahi or other lean fish fillets
2 tablespoons olive oil
2 tablespoons margarine or butter
½ cup chopped fennel bulb
¼ cup chopped onion (about 1 small)
¼ teaspoon salt
⅛ teaspoon pepper

Heat oven to 450°. If fish fillets are large, cut into 6 serving pieces. Arrange fish in ungreased rectangular baking dish, 12 × 7½ × 2 inches. Heat oil and margarine in 1-quart saucepan over medium-high heat. Sauté remaining ingredients in oil about 2 minutes. Spoon over fish. Bake 12 to 17 minutes or until fish flakes easily with fork. **6 servings**

PER SERVING: Calories 130; Protein 20 g; Carbohydrate 0 g; Fat 5 g; Cholesterol 35 mg; Sodium 90 mg

MICROWAVE DIRECTIONS: Arrange fish fillets, thickest parts to outside edges, in rectangular microwavable dish, 12 × 7½ × 2 inches. Place remaining ingredients in 4-cup microwavable measure. Cover fennel mixture tightly and microwave on high 2 minutes, stirring after 1 minute. Spoon over fish. Cover fish tightly and microwave 8 to 10 minutes, rotating dish ½ turn after 4 minutes, until fish flakes easily with fork. Let stand covered 3 minutes.

Salmon Steaks with Asparagus and Peas

4 small salmon or halibut steaks, each about 1 inch thick (about 1½ pounds)
½ teaspoon salt
½ teaspoon dried rosemary leaves, crushed
¼ cup water
1 tablespoon lemon juice
½ pound asparagus, cut into 2-inch pieces
1 cup fresh or frozen green peas
Lemon wedges

Arrange fish steaks in 10-inch skillet; sprinkle with salt and rosemary. Pour water and lemon juice into skillet. Heat to boiling; reduce heat. Cover and cook until fish is firm, about 8 minutes.

Arrange asparagus and peas on fish in skillet. Cover and simmer until vegetables are crisp-tender and fish flakes easily with fork, about 6 minutes. Remove fish and vegetables with slotted spoon. Serve with lemon wedges.

4 servings

PER SERVING: Calories 240; Protein 33 g; Carbohydrate 7 g; Fat 9 g; Cholesterol 55 mg; Sodium 360 mg

MICROWAVE DIRECTIONS: Arrange fish teaks in square microwavable dish, 8 × 8 × 2 inches. Sprinkle with salt, rosemary and lemon juice. Arrange asparagus and peas on fish. Cover with vented plastic wrap and microwave on high 5 minutes; rotate dish ½ turn. Microwave until fish flakes easily with fork and vegetables are crisp-tender, 4 to 5 minutes longer. Serve with lemon wedges.

Salmon Steaks with Asparagus and Peas

Salmon with Dilled Cucumbers

4 salmon or halibut steaks, ¾ inch thick (about 1½ pounds)
1 tablespoon chopped fresh or ½ teaspoon dried dill weed
¼ teaspoon salt
¼ cup water
1 tablespoon lemon juice
Dilled Cucumbers (below)

Place fish steaks in 10-inch nonstick skillet. Sprinkle with dill weed and salt. Pour water and lemon juice into skillet. Heat to boiling; reduce heat. Cover and cook 15 to 20 minutes or until fish flakes easily. Meanwhile, prepare Dilled Cucumbers. Serve over fish. **4 servings**

PER SERVING: Calories 205; Protein 36 g; Carbohydrate 4 g; Fat 4 g; Cholesterol 35 mg; Sodium 370 mg

Dilled Cucumbers

1 medium pared cucumber
1 tablespoon chopped fresh or 1 teaspoon dried dill weed
1 tablespoon vinegar
1½ teaspoons sugar
¼ teaspoon salt

Cut cucumber lengthwise into halves; seed and cut into thin slices. Mix cucumber and remaining ingredients in 1½-quart saucepan. Cook over high heat 1 to 2 minutes, stirring frequently, until cucumber is crisp-tender.

MICROWAVE DIRECTIONS: Arrange fish steaks, thickest parts to outside edges, in rectangular microwavable dish, 12 × 7½ × 2 inches. Sprinkle with dill weed and salt. Pour water and lemon juice over fish. Cover tightly and microwave on high 8 to 10 minutes, rotating dish ½ turn after 4 minutes, until fish flakes easily with fork. Let stand covered 3 minutes.

Prepare Dilled Cucumbers as directed—except place all ingredients in 1-quart microwavable casserole. Cover tightly and microwave on high 1 to 2 minutes or until cucumber is crisp-tender; drain. Serve over fish.

Microwaving Fish

Arrange fish fillets or steaks, thickest parts to outside edges, in shallow microwavable dish large enough to hold pieces in single layer. Cover tightly and microwave on high as directed below or until fish flakes easily with fork.

FISH	AMOUNT	TIME	STAND TIME
Fillets, ½ to ¾ inch thick	1 pound	5 to 7 minutes, rotating dish ½ turn after 3 minutes	2 minutes
	1½ pounds	7 to 9 minutes, rotating dish ½ turn after 4 minutes	3 minutes
Steaks, 1 inch thick	1 pound	5 to 7 minutes, rotating dish ½ turn after 3 minutes	3 minutes
	2 pounds	8 to 10 minutes, rotating dish, ½ turn after 4 minutes	3 minutes

Smoked Salmon Roulade

An easy oven omelet that's rolled, quick and elegant, without the work of individual omelets.

½ cup all-purpose flour
1 cup milk
3 tablespoons chopped green onion with tops
1 tablespoon chopped fresh or 1 teaspoon dried dill weed
2 tablespoons margarine or butter, melted
¼ teaspoon salt
4 eggs
1 cup flaked smoked salmon
1 package (10 ounces) frozen cut asparagus
1½ cups shredded Gruyère or Emmentaler cheese (6 ounces)

Heat oven to 350°. Line jelly roll pan, 15½ × 10½ × 1 inch, with aluminum foil. Grease foil generously. Beat flour, milk, onion, dill, margarine, salt and eggs until well blended. Pour into pan. Sprinkle with salmon. Bake 15 to 18 minutes or until eggs are set.

Meanwhile cook asparagus as directed on package; drain and keep warm. After removing eggs from oven, immediately sprinkle with cheese and asparagus. Roll up, beginning at narrow end, using foil to lift and roll roulade.   **6 servings**

PER SERVING: Calories 315; Protein 22 g; Carbohydrate 12 g; Fat 20 g; Cholesterol 220 mg; Sodium 405 mg

NOTE: 1 can (8 ounces) red salmon, drained and flaked, can be substituted for the smoked salmon.

HAM ROULADE: Substitute 1 cup coarsely chopped fully cooked smoked ham for the smoked salmon.

Salmon Hash

Leftover potatoes are a terrific excuse to make this delicious hash.

1 tablespoon vegetable oil
½ cup chopped onion (about 1 medium)
½ cup chopped green bell pepper (about 1 small)
½ cup chopped red bell pepper (about 1 small)
¼ teaspoon salt
⅛ teaspoon pepper
1 clove garlic, crushed
2 cups diced cooked potatoes (about 2 medium)
1 can (16 ounces) salmon, drained and flaked
Lemon wedges

Heat oil in 10-inch nonstick skillet over medium-high heat. Sauté onion, bell peppers, salt, pepper and garlic in oil. Stir in potatoes and salmon. Cook uncovered, stirring frequently, until hot. Serve with lemon wedges.   **4 servings**

PER SERVING: Calories 270; Protein 21 g; Carbohydrate 23 g; Fat 10 g; Cholesterol 40 mg; Sodium 460 mg

Sole with Red Grapes

1½ pounds sole fillets
1¼ cups water
⅓ cup dry white wine or chicken broth
1 tablespoon lemon juice
½ teaspoon salt
¼ teaspoon pepper
3 green onions (with tops), sliced
½ cup whipping (heavy) cream
2 tablespoons all-purpose flour
1 cup seedless red or green grapes

If fish fillets are large, cut into 6 serving pieces. Place fish in 10-inch skillet; add water, wine, lemon juice, salt, pepper and onions. Heat to boiling; reduce heat. Cover and simmer until fish flakes easily with fork, 5 to 6 minutes. Remove fish with slotted spatula; keep warm.

Shake whipping cream and flour in tightly covered container; stir into liquid in skillet. Heat to boiling. Continue boiling, stirring frequently, until slightly thickened, about 10 minutes. Add grapes; heat until hot. Spoon sauce over fish. **6 servings**

PER SERVING: Calories 185; Protein 20 g; Carbohydrate 8 g; Fat 8 g; Cholesterol 75 mg; Sodium 270 mg

MICROWAVE DIRECTIONS: Decrease water to ¾ cup and wine to ¼ cup. Arrange fish, with thickest parts to outside edges, in rectangular microwavable dish, 11 × 7 × 1½ inches. Sprinkle with lemon juice, salt, pepper and onions. Cover with plastic wrap, folding back one corner to vent, and microwave on high 4 minutes; rotate dish ½ turn. Microwave until fish flakes easily with fork, 3 to 4 minutes longer. Let stand covered.

Place water and wine in 4-cup microwavable measure. Shake whipping cream and flour in tightly covered container; gradually stir into wine mixture. Microwave uncovered on high to boiling, 3 to 4 minutes, stirring every minute. Stir in grapes. Serve sauce over fish.

Mediterranean-style Sole

4 sole fillets (about 1¼ pounds)
½ cup all-purpose flour
2 eggs, beaten
1 cup Italian-style dry bread crumbs
1 tablespoon chopped fresh sage leaves
1 tablespoon chopped fresh rosemary leaves
¼ cup butter or margarine (½ stick)
½ cup dry white wine or chicken broth
3 tablespoons lemon juice

Pat sole fillets dry. Coat fish with flour; dip into eggs. Coat with bread crumbs.

Cook sage and rosemary in butter in 12-inch skillet over low heat, stirring occasionally, 6 minutes. Add fish; cook uncovered over medium heat 4 minutes. Turn fish carefully. Add wine and lemon juice. Cook about 5 minutes longer or until fish flakes easily with fork. **4 servings**

PER SERVING: Calories 410; Protein 32 g; Carbohydrate 32 g; Fat 17 g; Cholesterol 205 mg; Sodium 400 mg

Gingered Tuna Steaks

Pompano, lake trout and mackerel are also delicious in this dish.

¼ cup margarine or butter, melted
1 tablespoon dry sherry or soy sauce
1 tablespoon soy sauce
1 tablespoon grated gingerroot
6 small albacore tuna or other fatty fish steaks, about 1 inch thick (about 2 pounds)

Mix margarine, sherry, soy sauce and gingerroot. Set oven control to broil. Brush fish steaks with half the margarine mixture. Broil fish with tops about 4 inches from heat 9 minutes. Turn fish carefully and brush with remaining margarine mixture. Broil about 9 minutes or until fish flakes easily with fork.   **6 servings**

PER SERVING: Calories 265; Protein 33 g; Carbohydrate 0 g; Fat 13 g; Cholesterol 55 mg; Sodium 360 mg

Oven-poached Halibut

Oven-poaching is low-calorie as well as easy.

    4 halibut steaks, 1 inch thick (about 1½ pounds)
    ¼ teaspoon salt
    4 sprigs dill weed
    4 slices lemon
    5 black peppercorns
    ¼ cup dry white wine or water

Heat oven to 450°. Place fish steaks in ungreased rectangular baking dish, 12 × 7½ × 2 inches. Sprinkle with salt. Place dill weed sprig and lemon slice on each. Top with peppercorns. Pour wine over fish. Bake uncovered 20 to 25 minutes or until fish flakes easily.   **4 servings**

PER SERVING: Calories 200; Protein 35 g; Carbohydrate 1 g; Fat 4 g; Cholesterol 55 mg; Sodium 230 mg

MICROWAVE DIRECTIONS: Prepare as directed— except arrange fish steaks, thickest parts to outside edges, in rectangular microwavable dish, 12 × 7½ × 2 inches. Cover tightly and microwave on high 7 to 9 minutes, rotating dish ½ turn after 4 minutes, until fish flakes easily with fork. Let stand covered 3 minutes; drain.

Sea Bass with Green Beans

½ pound sea bass or walleye fillet
1 teaspoon cornstarch
1 teaspoon sesame oil
½ teaspoon salt
½ teaspoon finely chopped gingerroot
Dash of white pepper
10 ounces green beans
1 green onion (with top)
1 tablespoon cornstarch
1 tablespoon water
1 teaspoon sugar
¼ teaspoon sesame oil
4 tablespoons vegetable oil
1 teaspoon finely chopped garlic
½ teaspoon salt
½ cup chicken broth

Cut fish into 2 × ½-inch slices. Toss fish, 1 teaspoon cornstarch, 1 teaspoon sesame oil, ½ teaspoon salt, the gingerroot and white pepper in medium glass or pastic bowl. Cover and refrigerate 20 minutes.

Snap green beans into halves. Cut onion diagonally into 1-inch pieces. Mix 1 tablespoon cornstarch and the water. Mix sugar and ¼ teaspoon sesame oil.

Heat wok or 12-inch skillet until very hot. Add 2 tablespoons vegetable oil; rotate wok to coat side. Add fish; stir-fry gently 2 minutes or until fish turns white. Remove fish from wok.

Heat wok until very hot. Add remaining 2 tablespoons vegetable oil; rotate wok to coat side. Add beans, garlic and ½ teaspoon salt; stir-fry 1 minute. Add broth; heat to boiling. Cover and cook 2 minutes. Stir in cornstarch mixture; cook and stir until mixture thickens. Add fish and onion; cook and stir gently 30 seconds or until fish is hot. Gently stir in the sesame oil mixture.   **4 servings**

PER SERVING: Calories 225; Protein 12 g; Carbohydrate 9 g; Fat 16 g; Cholesterol 50 mg; Sodium 680 mg

**Trout and Spinach Salad with Chutney
Dressing**

Trout and Spinach Salad with Chutney Dressing

Chutney Dressing (below)
3 cups bite-size pieces spinach (about 6 ounces)
1 cup sliced fresh mushrooms (about 3 ounces)
½ cup bean sprouts
2 thin slices red onion, separated into rings
1 pound lake trout or other fatty fish fillets, skinned

Prepare Chutney Dressing. Toss spinach, mushrooms, bean sprouts, onion and half of the dressing. Place on 4 serving plates.

Set oven control to broil. Cut fish fillets into 4 serving pieces. Place on rack in broiler pan. Broil with tops about 4 inches from heat 5 to 6 minutes or until fish flakes easily with fork (do not turn). Place fish on spinach mixture. Pour remaining dressing over fish. Serve with freshly ground pepper if desired. **4 servings**

PER SERVING: Calories 240; Protein 26 g; Carbohydrate 15 g; Fat 8 g; Cholesterol 65 mg; Sodium 170 mg

Chutney Dressing

⅓ cup chutney, chopped if necessary
1 tablespoon vegetable oil
1 tablespoon lemon juice
⅛ teaspoon salt

Shake all ingredients in tightly covered container.

Dilled Pasta Salad with Smoked Fish

An unusual salad, thanks to the smoky tang of the fish.

2 cups uncooked rotini or spiral pasta
½ cup mayonnaise or salad dressing
¼ cup plain yogurt or sour cream
1 tablespoon chopped fresh or ½ teaspoon dried dill weed
½ teaspoon dry mustard
¼ teaspoon salt
¼ teaspoon pepper
1 can (2¼ ounces) sliced pitted ripe olives, drained (about ½ cup)
2 green onions (with tops), thinly sliced
1 medium zucchini, thinly sliced (about 2 cups)
1 medium carrot, thinly sliced (about ½ cup)
2 cups flaked boneless smoked whitefish or salmon (about ⅔ pound)

Cook rotini as directed on package; drain. Rinse pasta in cold water; drain. Mix mayonnaise, yogurt, dill weed, mustard, salt and pepper in large bowl. Add rotini and remaining ingredients except smoked fish; toss. Gently stir in smoked fish. **4 servings**

PER SERVING: Calories 415; Protein 24 g; Carbohydrate 21 g; Fat 26 g; Cholesterol 95 mg; Sodium 1,140 mg

Tuna–Bean Salad

3 cans (15 ounces each) cannellini beans
  or great northern beans, drained
1 jar (2 ounces) diced pimientos, drained
1 large green bell pepper, chopped
  (about 1 cup)
1 medium onion, chopped (about 1/2 cup)
1/4 cup chopped fresh parsley
1/4 cup olive or vegetable oil
2 tablespoons lemon juice
2 tablespoons capers
1/4 teaspoon red pepper sauce
Lettuce leaves
1 can (6 1/2 ounces) tuna in water, drained

Mix beans, pimientos, bell pepper, onion and
parsley. Shake oil, lemon juice, capers and pepper sauce in tightly covered container. Toss with
bean mixture. Spoon onto lettuce. Top with tuna.
Serve with lemon wedges if desired.

5 servings

PER SERVING: Calories 350; Protein 22 g; Carbohydrate 41 g; Fat 12 g; Cholesterol 20 mg; Sodium 280 mg

South Seas Shrimp Salad

*You can make your own five-spice powder
by mixing 1 teaspoon ground cinnamon, 1
star anise or 1 teaspoon anise seed, 1 teaspoon fennel seed, 1/4 teaspoon peppercorns and 1/4 teaspoon ground cloves in a
blender. Blend on high speed until finely
ground. Store powder in a tightly covered
container.*

2 cups bite-size pieces spinach
2 cups shredded Chinese cabbage
8 ounces cooked cleaned shrimp (about
  1 1/2 cups)
1 cup enoki mushrooms
1/4 cup slivered almonds, toasted
1 red bell pepper, cut into 1/2-inch pieces
1 green onion (with top), thinly sliced
  (about 1 tablespoon)
2 tablespoons vegetable oil
2 tablespoons rice vinegar or vinegar
2 tablespoons soy sauce
1/2 teaspoon five-spice powder

Mix spinach, cabbage, shrimp, mushrooms, almonds, bell pepper and onion. Shake remaining
ingredients in tightly covered container. Pour
over spinach mixture and toss.   **4 servings**

PER SERVING: Calories 180; Protein 11 g; Carbohydrate 7 g; Fat 13 g; Cholesterol 115 mg; Sodium 625 mg

---

SOUTH SEAS CHICKEN SALAD: Substitute 1 1/4 cups
cut-up cooked chicken for the shrimp and 2 tablespoons sesame seeds, toasted, for the
almonds.

Shrimp Cilantro

Cilantro adds a southwestern flavor to these shrimp.

1 medium onion, chopped (about ½ cup)
2 cloves garlic, finely chopped
2 tablespoons margarine or butter
2 tablespoons vegetable oil
16 large raw shrimp, peeled and deveined
2 tablespoons snipped fresh cilantro
Lemon slices

Cook and stir onion and garlic in margarine and oil in 10-inch skillet until tender. Add shrimp; cook 1 minute.

Turn shrimp; cook until pink, about 2 minutes longer. (Do not overcook.) Remove shrimp to serving dish; sprinkle with cilantro. Pour pan juices over shrimp; serve with lemon slices.

4 servings

PER SERVING: Calories 155; Protein 6 g; Carbohydrate 3 g; Fat 13 g; Cholesterol 55 mg; Sodium 130 mg

Shrimp Fajitas

8 flour tortillas (7 or 8 inches in diameter)
1 tablespoon vegetable oil
1 pound raw medium shrimp, peeled and deveined
1 tablespoon lime juice
1½ teaspoons chopped fresh or ½ teaspoon dried oregano leaves
¼ teaspoon ground cumin
1 clove garlic, finely chopped
1 cup chunky red salsa
1 cup guacamole

Heat oven to 250°. Wrap tortillas in aluminum foil or place on heat-proof serving plate and cover with aluminum foil. Heat in oven for about 15 minutes or until warm.

Heat oil in 10-inch skillet over medium heat. Add shrimp, lime juice, oregano, cumin and garlic. Cook about 5 minutes, stirring constantly, until shrimp are pink.

Divide shrimp evenly among tortillas. Top with salsa and guacamole. Fold one end of tortilla up about 1 inch over shrimp mixture. Fold right and left sides over folded end, overlapping. Fold down remaining end. Serve with extra salsa and guacamole if desired. **4 servings**

PER SERVING: Calories 470; Protein 25 g; Carbohydrate 57 g; Fat 16 g; Cholesterol 170 mg; Sodium 1,390 mg

Shrimp Étouffée

A wondeful time-saving version of this classic New Orleans dish.

1 pound fresh or frozen medium raw
 shrimp (in shells)
¼ cup margarine or butter (½ stick)
3 tablespoons all-purpose flour
1 medium onion, chopped (about ½ cup)
1 small green bell pepper, chopped
 (about ½ cup)
1 medium stalk celery, sliced (about ½
 cup)
1 clove garlic, finely chopped
1 cup water
2 tablespoons snipped fresh parsley
2 teaspoons lemon juice
½ teaspoon salt
¼ teaspoon pepper
⅛ to ¼ teaspoon red pepper sauce
2 cups hot cooked rice

Peel shrimp. Make a shallow cut lengthwise down back of each shrimp and wash out vein.

Heat margarine in 3-quart saucepan over medium heat until melted. Stir in flour. Cook about 6 minutes, stirring constantly, until bubbly and brown. Stir in onion, bell pepper, celery and garlic. Cook and stir about 5 minutes or until vegetables are crisp-tender.

Stir in shrimp, water, parsley, lemon juice, salt, pepper and pepper sauce. Heat to boiling; reduce heat. Simmer uncovered about 5 minutes, stirring occasionally, until shrimp are pink. Serve over rice.   **4 servings**

PER SERVING: Calories 290; Protein 11 g; Carbohydrate 33 g; Fat 12 g; Cholesterol 55 mg; Sodium 825 mg

CRAWFISH ÉTOUFFÉE: Substitute cleaned raw crawfish for the shrimp. (Sizes of crawfish vary depending on region and variety; 40 to 48 crawfish, each about 5 inches long, yield about 1 pound tail meat.)

Grilled Shrimp and Scallop Kabobs

¼ cup lemon juice
¼ cup vegetable oil
1 tablespoon chopped fresh or 1 teaspoon dried thyme leaves
¼ teaspoon salt
¼ teaspoon pepper
¾ pound sea scallops
12 raw large shrimp (in shells)
8 medium whole mushrooms (about
 6 ounces)
8 cherry tomatoes
1 medium zucchini (about 1 inch in diameter), cut into 1-inch slices

Mix lemon juice, oil, thyme, salt and pepper. Cut scallops into halves if over 1 inch in diameter. Arrange scallops, shrimp and vegetables alternately on four 10-inch metal skewers. Brush with lemon-thyme mixture. Grill 4 inches from medium coals 10 to 15 minutes, brushing with mixture frequently, until scallops are opaque in center and shrimp are pink.   **4 servings**

PER SERVING: Calories 215; Protein 25 g; Carbohydrate 8 g; Fat 9 g; Cholesterol 65 mg; Sodium 410 mg

Grilled Shrimp and Scallop Kabobs

Quick Jambalaya

1 package (8 ounces) brown-and-serve
    sausage links
1½ cups uncooked instant rice
1½ cups water
1 can (14½ ounces) stewed tomatoes,
    undrained
1 package (10 ounces) frozen quick-
    cooking shrimp
1 small onion, chopped (about ¼ cup)
½ medium green bell pepper, chopped
2 teaspoons instant chicken bouillon
1 teaspoon chopped fresh or ¼ teaspoon
    dried thyme leaves
¼ teaspoon chile powder
⅛ teaspoon ground red pepper (cayenne)

Cut sausages into 1-inch diagonal slices. Cook
in 10-inch skillet according to package directions; drain. Add remaining ingredients to skillet. Heat to boiling, stirring occasionally;
reduce heat. Simmer uncovered 10 minutes,
stirring occasionally.   **4 servings**

PER SERVING: Calories 490; Protein 27 g; Carbohydrate 48 g; Fat 21 g; Cholesterol 150 mg; Sodium 1,120 mg

Scallops in Wine Sauce

*Can't find bay scallops? Use sea scallops.
Cut them into halves or fourths so they
are approximately ½ inch in diameter, and
the same cooking time can be used.*

1½ cups sliced mushrooms (about 4
    ounces)
1 small leek sliced, with green top (about
    ⅓ cup)
2 tablespoons reduced-calorie margarine
2 tablespoons olive or vegetable oil
½ cup dry white wine or chicken broth
½ teaspoon chopped fresh or ⅛ teaspoon
    dried tarragon leaves
1 pound bay scallops
2 teaspoons cornstarch
2 tablespoons cold water
3 cups shredded lettuce
1 lemon, cut into wedges

Cook mushrooms and leek in margarine and oil
in 10-inch skillet 5 minutes, stirring occasionally.
Stir in wine and tarragon. Heat to boiling. Stir in
scallops; reduce heat. Cook uncovered 3 to 4
minutes, stirring occasionally, until scallops are
white.

Mix cornstarch and water; stir into scallop mixture. Heat to boiling, stirring constantly. Boil and
stir 1 minute. Spoon scallop mixture over lettuce;
garnish with lemon.   **4 servings**

PER SERVING: Calories 330; Protein 28 g; Carbohydrate 10 g; Fat 14 g; Cholesterol 60 mg; Sodium 380 mg

Scallops with Broccoli and Mushrooms

1 pound scallops
4 ounces mushrooms, sliced (about 1½ cups)
2 tablespoons margarine or butter
2 cups cut-up broccoli or 1 package (10 ounces) frozen chopped broccoli, thawed
1 jar (2 ounces) sliced pimientos, drained
1 can (10¾ ounces) condensed chicken broth
3 tablespoons cornstarch
2 teaspoons soy sauce
Hot cooked rice or pasta

If scallops are large, cut into halves. Cook and stir mushrooms in margarine in 3-quart saucepan over medium heat until tender, about 5 minutes. Stir in scallops, broccoli and pimientos. Cook, stirring frequently, until scallops are white, 3 to 4 minutes.

Gradually stir chicken broth into cornstarch until smooth. Stir broth mixture and soy sauce into scallop mixture. Heat to boiling, stirring constantly. Boil and stir 1 minute. Serve over rice. **4 servings**

PER SERVING: Calories 385; Protein 33 g; Carbohydrate 43 g; Fat 9 g; Cholesterol 35 mg; Sodium 1,420 mg

Curried Scallops

3 tablespoons margarine or butter
1 pound sea scallops, cut into halves
3 green onions (with tops), chopped
1 tablespoon all-purpose flour
1 tablespoon curry powder
½ teaspoon salt
½ cup chicken broth
½ cup milk
1 medium tomato, chopped (about ½ cup)
3 cups hot cooked rice

Heat 1 tablespoon of the margarine in 10-inch skillet over medium-high heat until melted. Cook scallops in margarine 4 to 5 minutes, stirring frequently, until scallops are white. Remove from skillet; drain skillet.

Heat remaining 2 tablespoons margarine in same skillet. Cook onions, flour, curry powder and salt over medium heat, stirring constantly, until bubbly; remove from heat. Stir in broth and milk. Heat to boiling, stirring constantly. Boil and stir 1 minute. Stir in tomato and scallops. Heat about 3 minutes, stirring occasionally. Serve over rice. **6 servings**

PER SERVING: Calories 230; Protein 12 g; Carbohydrate 30 g; Fat 7 g; Cholesterol 20 mg; Sodium 810 mg

Stir-Fried Scallops and Pea Pods

Stir-fried Scallops and Pea Pods

Great served over white or brown rice!

1 pound scallops
1 tablespoon packed brown sugar
1 tablespoon soy sauce
2 teaspoons cornstarch
6 slices bacon, cut into 1-inch pieces
6 green onions (with tops), cut into 1-inch pieces
1 can (8 ounces) sliced water chestnuts, drained
4 ounces fresh Chinese pea pods or 1 package (6 ounces) frozen Chinese pea pods, thawed

If scallops are large, cut into halves. Toss scallops, brown sugar, soy sauce and cornstarch in bowl; cover and refrigerate 10 minutes.

Cook and stir bacon in 10-inch skillet or wok over medium heat until crisp. Drain, reserving 1 tablespoon fat in skillet; reserve bacon.

Cook and stir scallops, onions and water chestnuts in bacon fat over medium-high heat until scallops are white, about 7 minutes; stir in pea pods. Stir in bacon just before serving.

4 servings

PER SERVING: Calories 280; Protein 30 g; Carbohydrate 19 g; Fat 9 g; Cholesterol 45 mg; Sodium 760 mg

Stir-fried Crabmeat with Celery Cabbage

10 ounces frozen cooked crabmeat, thawed
½ pound celery cabbage
2 green onions (with tops)
1 tablespoon cornstarch
1 tablespoon water
1 teaspoon sugar
1 teaspoon sesame oil
3 tablespoons vegetable oil
1 teaspoon finely chopped gingerroot
1 teaspoon finely chopped garlic
½ teaspoon salt
½ cup chicken broth

Drain crabmeat thoroughly; remove cartilage. Squeeze out excess moisture. Cut celery cabbage into 1-inch pieces. Cut onions diagonally into 1-inch pieces. Mix cornstarch, water, sugar and sesame oil.

Heat wok or 12-inch skillet until very hot. Add vegetable oil; rotate wok to coat side. Add gingerroot and garlic; stir-fry 30 seconds. Add celery cabbage and salt; stir-fry 1 minute.

Add broth; heat to boiling. Cover and cook 2 minutes over high heat. Stir in cornstarch mixture; cook and stir until thickened. Stir in crabmeat and onions; cook and stir 1 minute or until crabmeat is hot.

4 servings

PER SERVING: Calories 190; Protein 15 g; Carbohydrate 5 g; Fat 13 g; Cholesterol 40 mg; Sodium 1170 mg

Tarragon–Seafood Salad

Tarragon–Seafood Salad

3 cups uncooked bow-shaped pasta (about 6 ounces)
4 ounces pea pods, cut into halves
2 tablespoons olive or vegetable oil
1 tablespoon chopped fresh or 1 teaspoon dried tarragon leaves
1/2 teaspoon salt
1/4 teaspoon white pepper
2 cloves garlic, finely chopped
3/4 pound seafood sticks, cut into 1/2-inch pieces

Cook pasta as directed on package—except add pea pods 1 minute before pasta is done; drain. Rinse pasta and pea pods in cold water; drain. Gently toss all ingredients.   **4 servings**

PER SERVING: Calories 310; Protein 19 g; Carbohydrate 41 g; Fat 8 g; Cholesterol 25 mg; Sodium 1,170 mg

Great Pasta Salads

Pasta salads are a wonderful quick dinner. Follow these tips for easy pasta salads.

• Cook pasta in water to which you have added some oil. This makes the pasta more slippery, perfect for salads.

• Water should be at a full boil when you add pasta, and should remain at a boil during the entire cooking period.

• After cooking, rinse pasta in cold water. This allows you to make a pasta salad without extra chilling time.

• If you want to cook vegetables for the salad, add them directly to the pasta and water about one minute before pasta is cooked. (See Tarragon–Seafood Salad, above)

Steamed Mussels in Wine Sauce

24 large mussels (about 2 pounds)
2 tablespoons olive oil
1/2 cup snipped fresh parsley
4 cloves garlic, finely chopped
1 cup dry white wine or chicken broth
1/2 teaspoon salt
1/2 teaspoon pepper

Discard any broken-shell or open (dead) mussels. Wash remaining mussels, removing any barnacles with a dull paring knife. Remove beards by tugging them away from shells.

Heat oil in 12-inch skillet over medium-high heat. Sauté parsley and garlic in oil. Add mussels, wine, salt and pepper. Cover and cook 10 minutes. Discard unopened mussels. Drizzle liquid from skillet over each serving.   **4 servings**

PER SERVING: Calories 160; Protein 16 g; Carbohydrate 6 g; Fat 8 g; Cholesterol 40 mg; Sodium 620 mg

Home-style Scrambled Eggs

4

Meatless Meals

═══════════════ ▣ ═══════════════

Home-style Scrambled Eggs

4 eggs
3 tablespoons water
½ teaspoon salt
2 tablespoons margarine or butter
3 tablespoons finely chopped onion
1 medium potato, cooked and cubed (about 1 cup)
1 medium tomato, seeded and chopped
1 small zucchini, chopped

Beat eggs, water and salt with fork; set aside. Heat margarine in 10-inch skillet over medium heat until melted. Cook and stir vegetables in margarine 2 minutes. Pour egg mixture into skillet.

As mixture begins to set at bottom and side, gently lift cooked portions with spatula so that thin, uncooked portion can flow to bottom. Avoid constant stirring. Cook 3 to 5 minutes or until eggs are thickened throughout but still moist. **4 servings**

PER SERVING: Calories 160; Protein 7 g; Carbohydrate 8 g; Fat 11 g; Cholesterol 215 mg; Sodium 400 mg

Southwestern Eggs

Chihuahua cheese takes its name from the Mexican state in which it originated. It has the creamy texture and tang of Cheddar, but melts like mozzarella. For a lighter dish, try the eggs without sausage.

1 pound bulk pork sausage
½ cup chopped onion (about 1 medium)
1 large green bell pepper, cut into 1-inch pieces
1¼ cups prepared red chunky salsa
4 eggs
¾ cup shredded Chihuahua or mozzarella cheese (3 ounces)

Cook sausage, onion and bell pepper in 10-inch skillet over medium heat, stirring occasionally, until sausage is brown; drain. Stir in salsa; heat until hot. Spread mixture evenly in skillet. Make 4 indentations in mixture with back of spoon. Break 1 egg into each indentation. Cover and cook over low heat about 12 minutes or until whites are set and yolks are thickened. Sprinkle with cheese. Serve with sour cream if desired. **4 servings**

PER SERVING: Calories 380; Protein 17 g; Carbohydrate 16 g; Fat 28 g; Cholesterol 275 mg; Sodium 1185 mg

Huevos Rancheros

Huevos rancheros *("ranch-style eggs")* re-fers to any egg dish served on tortillas. *Spicy sausage makes this version a hearty one. If you prefer, you can leave out the sausage.*

8 ounces bulk chorizo sausage
Vegetable oil
6 corn tortillas (6 to 7 inches in diameter)
1½ cups warm salsa
6 fried eggs
1½ cups shredded Cheddar cheese (6 ounces)

Cook and stir sausage until done; drain. Heat ⅛ inch oil in 8-inch skillet over medium heat just until hot. Cook tortillas, one at a time, in oil until crisp, about 1 minute; drain.

Spread each tortilla with 1 tablespoon Casera Sauce to soften. Place 1 egg on each tortilla; top each with scant tablespoon Casera Sauce, ¼ cup sausage, another tablespoon sauce and ¼ cup cheese. **6 servings**

PER SERVING: Calories 550; Protein 25 g; Carbohydrate 16 g; Fat 43 g; Cholesterol 275 mg; Sodium 950 mg

Festival Eggs

¼ cup margarine or butter
¼ cup vegetable oil
6 flour tortillas (7 to 8 inches in diameter), cut into thin strips
1 medium onion, chopped (about ½ cup)
6 eggs, beaten
2 medium tomatoes, chopped (about 2 cups)
1 jalapeño chile, seeded and chopped
2 tablespoons snipped fresh cilantro
¾ teaspoon salt
¼ teaspoon pepper
½ cup shredded Colby cheese (2 ounces)

Heat margarine and oil in 10-inch skillet over medium heat until hot. Add tortilla strips and onion; cook, turning occasionally, until tortillas are brown.

Mix remaining ingredients except cheese; pour into skillet. As mixture begins to set at bottom and side, gently lift cooked portions with spatula so that thin uncooked portion can flow to bottom. Avoid constant stirring. Turn egg mixture; cook until eggs are cooked throughout but still moist, 3 to 5 minutes. Sprinkle with cheese.

6 servings

PER SERVING: Calories 420; Protein 13 g; Carbohydrate 29 g; Fat 28 g; Cholesterol 225 mg; Sodium 640 mg

Eggs Florentine

This French dish, with a traditional Mornay Sauce (a white sauce flavored with cheese), is lovely for a simple dinner.

1 package (10 ounces) frozen chopped spinach
Mornay Sauce (below)
4 Poached Eggs (right)
2 tablespoons grated Parmesan cheese
1 tablespoon dry bread crumbs

Cook spinach as directed on package; drain. Place spinach in ungreased shallow 1-quart baking dish; keep warm. Prepare Mornay Sauce and Poached Eggs. Place eggs on spinach. Cover with Mornay Sauce; sprinkle with cheese and bread crumbs. Set oven control to broil or 550°. Broil with top about 5 inches from heat until light brown, about 1 minute.

4 servings

PER SERVING: Calories 215; Protein 12 g; Carbohydrate 8 g; Fat 15 g; Cholesterol 240 mg; Sodium 220 mg

Mornay Sauce

2 teaspoons margarine or butter
2 teaspoons all-purpose flour
½ teaspoon instant chicken bouillon
Dash of ground nutmeg
Dash of ground red pepper (cayenne)
¾ cup half-and-half
¼ cup shredded Swiss cheese

Heat margarine in 1-quart saucepan until melted. Blend in flour, bouillon (dry), nutmeg and red pepper. Cook over low heat, stirring constantly, until mixture is smooth and bubbly. Stir in half-and-half. Heat to boiling, stirring constantly.

Boil and stir 1 minute. Add cheese; stir until cheese is melted.

POACHED EGGS: Heat water (1½ to 2 inches) to boiling; reduce to simmer. Break each egg into saucer; holding saucer close to water's surface, slip 1 egg at a time into water. Cook until desired doneness, 3 to 5 minutes. Remove eggs from water with slotted spoon.

Quick Eggs and Cheese

Eggs and cheese are great to have on hand for tasty dinners in minutes. You'll find these tips useful when you are rushed for time:

• Keep hard-cooked eggs on hand to make sandwiches or to top salads, vegetables or sauces.

• For an egg sandwich on the run, serve egg salad or scrambled eggs in a tortilla or pita bread.

• For a quick light meal, set out a platter of assorted cheeses, fresh fruit and crackers, and let people serve themselves.

• For a quick toasted-cheese sandwich, use the microwave. Place cheese between 2 slices of toasted bread. Microwave on microwavable paper towel for about 1 minute on medium (50%).

• Make a quick fondue with cheese soup thinned with wine or beer.

• Vary cottage cheese by stirring in one of these easy combinations: shredded carrots and raisins; crushed pineapple and fresh mint; chopped green bell pepper, tomato and onion; sunflower nuts, alfalfa sprouts and chopped carrots; toasted pine nuts, chopped tomato and basil.

Blue Cheese Omelet with Pears

Blue Cheese Omelet with Pears

Pears and blue cheese are a wonderful combination in this fresh-tasting omelet.

4 eggs
1 tablespoon margarine or butter
¼ cup crumbled Danish blue cheese or Gorgonzola cheese
1 tablespoon snipped chives
1 unpared pear, cut into wedges

Mix eggs with fork just until whites and yolks are blended. Heat margarine in 8-inch skillet or omelet pan over medium-high heat just until margarine begins to brown. As margarine melts, tilt skillet to coat bottom completely.

Quickly pour eggs, all at once, into skillet. Slide skillet back and forth rapidly over heat and, at the same time, stir quickly with fork to spread eggs continuously over bottom of pan as they thicken. Let stand over heat a few seconds to lightly brown bottom of omelet. (Do not over-cook—omelet will continue to cook after folding.)

Tilt skillet; run fork under edge of omelet, then jerk skillet sharply to loosen eggs from bottom of skillet. Sprinkle with blue cheese and chives. Fold portion of omelet nearest you just to center. (Allow for portion of omelet to slide up side of skillet.)

Grasp skillet handle; turn omelet onto warm plate, flipping folded portion of omelet over so far side is on bottom. Serve with pear wedges.

2 servings

PER SERVING: Calories 310; Protein 16 g; Carbohydrate 14 g; Fat 21 g; Cholesterol 440 mg; Sodium 430 mg

Omelet Tips

Omelets are great quick dinners, especially when you add cheese, vegetables or left-over meat. Below are some sure-fire omelet techniques.

Tilt pan and run fork under edge of omelet, then jerk skillet sharply to loosen eggs from bottom of skillet. Fold portion of omelet just to center.

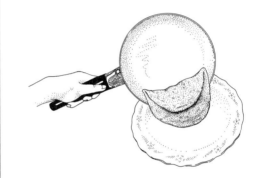

Turn omelet onto plate, flipping folded portion of omelet over so it is on the bottom.

Malaysian Omelet

The peanut oil here will not brown excessively as butter and margarine often do with long cooking. Serve this thin omelet in wedges, as Malaysians do.

2 cups mixed thinly sliced eggplant, green pepper and onion
1 tablespoon peanut oil
1 medium onion, finely chopped (about ½ cup)
1 green chile, seeded and finely chopped (about 1 tablespoon)
1 red chile, seeded and finely chopped (about 1 tablespoon)
1 clove garlic, finely chopped
2 tablespoons peanut oil
4 eggs, beaten
¼ teaspoon salt
¼ teaspoon pepper

Cook 2 cups vegetables in 1 tablespoon oil until tender; reserve.

Cook chopped onion, chiles and garlic in 2 tablespoons oil in 10-inch skillet until tender. Mix eggs, salt and pepper; pour into skillet. Cover and cook over low heat until eggs are set and light brown on bottom, about 8 minutes. Cut eggs into wedges; spoon reserved vegetable mixture over omelet. **4 servings**

PER SERVING: Calories 195; Protein 7 g; Carbohydrate 8 g; Fat 15 g; Cholesterol 215 mg; Sodium 200 mg

Vegetable Frittata

A frittata is an Italian omelet that is open-face, not folded like a French omelet.

3 tablespoons vegetable oil
½ cup sliced zucchini
1 small bell pepper, cut into ¼-inch strips
1 small onion, thinly sliced
1 clove garlic, finely chopped
½ cup coarsely chopped tomato
2 teaspoons chopped fresh or ½ teaspoon dried oregano leaves
2 teaspoons chopped fresh or ½ teaspoon dried basil leaves
8 eggs
½ teaspoon salt
¼ teaspoon pepper
½ cup shredded Fontina or mozzarella cheese (2 ounces)
2 tablespoons grated Romano or Parmesan cheese

Heat oil in 10-inch ovenproof skillet over medium heat. Cook zucchini, bell pepper, onion and garlic in oil 3 minutes, stirring occasionally. Stir in tomato, oregano and basil. Reduce heat to medium-low. Beat eggs, salt and pepper until blended. Stir in Fontina cheese. Pour over vegetable mixture. Cover and cook 9 to 11 minutes or until eggs are set around edge and light brown on bottom. Sprinkle with Romano cheese.

Set oven control to broil. Broil frittata with top about 5 inches from heat about 3 minutes or until golden brown. **6 servings**

PER SERVING: Calories 215; Protein 11 g; Carbohydrate 5 g; Fat 17 g; Cholesterol 375 mg; Sodium 10 mg

Broccoli and Swiss Cheese Frittata

1 medium onion, chopped (about ½ cup)
2 cloves garlic, finely chopped
2 tablespoons margarine or butter
1 tablespoon olive or vegetable oil
1 package (10 ounces) frozen chopped broccoli, thawed and drained
8 eggs
½ teaspoon salt
¼ teaspoon pepper
1 cup shredded Swiss cheese (4 ounces)
1 to 2 tablespoons snipped fresh or 1 teaspoon dried oregano leaves
2 tablespoons shredded Swiss cheese

Cook onion and garlic in margarine and oil in 10-inch ovenproof skillet over medium heat, stirring frequently, until onion is tender, about 5 minutes. Remove from heat; stir in broccoli.

Beat eggs, salt and pepper until blended; stir in 1 cup cheese and the oregano. Pour over broccoli mixture. Cover and cook over medium-low heat until eggs are set around edge and light brown on bottom, 9 to 11 minutes.

Set oven control to broil. Broil frittata with top about 5 inches from heat until golden brown, about 2 minutes. Sprinkle with 2 tablespoons cheese; cut into wedges. **6 servings**

PER SERVING: Calories 260; Protein 16 g; Carbohydrate 6 g; Fat 19 g; Cholesterol 305 mg; Sodium 370 mg

Egg Foo Yong

4 eggs
2 egg whites
1⅓ cups bean sprouts
¼ cup sliced green onions (with tops)
¼ teaspoon salt
Vegetable oil
Brown Sauce (below)

Beat eggs and egg whites until thick and lemon colored, about 5 minutes. Stir in bean sprouts, onions and salt. For each patty, lightly brush 10-inch nonstick skillet with oil. Heat over medium heat until hot.

Pour scant ¼ cup egg mixture at a time into skillet. Push cooked egg up over bean sprouts with broad spatula to form a patty. Cook until patty is set; turn. Cook over medium heat until other side is brown. Place on warm platter; keep warm. Prepare Brown Sauce; serve with egg patties. **4 servings**

PER SERVING: Calories 115; Protein 9 g; Carbohydrate 4 g; Fat 7 g; Cholesterol 275 mg; Sodium 750 mg

Brown Sauce

½ cup water
2 tablespoons soy sauce
1 teaspoon cornstarch
1 teaspoon sugar
1 teaspoon vinegar

Cook all ingredients until mixture thickens and boils, stirring constantly. Boil and stir 1 minute.

Curried Eggs and Vegetables on Rice

For this dish, you make your own curry; commercial curries vary widely.

8 ounces small whole mushrooms
1 cup finely chopped onion (about 1 large)
1 tablespoon reduced-calorie margarine
1 teaspoon salt
1 teaspoon ground coriander
1/2 teaspoon ground turmeric
1/2 teaspoon ground ginger
1/2 teaspoon ground cumin
3 medium tomatoes, cut into wedges
1/4 cup chicken broth
6 hard-cooked eggs
1 teaspoon lemon juice
2 cups hot cooked rice

Cook and stir mushrooms and onion in margarine in 10-inch nonstick skillet until onion is tender, about 5 minutes. Stir in salt, coriander, turmeric, ginger and cumin; cook and stir 1 minute. Stir in tomatoes and chicken broth. Heat to boiling; reduce heat. Simmer uncovered 5 minutes, stirring occasionally.

Cut eggs lengthwise into halves. Carefully place eggs yolk side up in skillet; spoon sauce over eggs. Simmer uncovered without stirring until eggs are hot, 3 to 5 minutes. Stir in lemon juice just before serving. Serve over rice.

4 servings

PER SERVING: Calories 305; Protein 14 g; Carbohydrate 37 g; Fat 11 g; Cholesterol 410 mg; Sodium 1160 mg

Tortellini in Balsamic Vinaigrette

Prepare Balsamic Vinaigrette and stir in the remaining ingredients while the tortellini cook. This gives the vegetables time to marinate; the dish can be finished quickly by stirring in the tortellini when they are cooked.

1 package (7 ounces) uncooked tricolor cheese tortellini
Balsamic Vinaigrette (below)
1 medium carrot, sliced
2 cups broccoli flowerets
2 green onions (with tops), sliced

Cook tortellini as directed on package; drain. Rinse with cold water; drain.

Prepare Balsamic Vinaigrette in large bowl. Stir in remaining ingredients, except tortellini. Stir in tortellini.

4 servings

PER SERVING: Calories 215; Protein 9 g; Carbohydrate 18 g; Fat 12 g; Cholesterol 70 mg; Sodium 210 mg

Balsamic Vinaigrette

1/4 cup balsamic or cider vinegar
2 tablespoons olive or vegetable oil
1 tablespoon chopped fresh or 1 teaspoon dried basil leaves
1/4 teaspoon paprika
1/8 teaspoon salt
1 clove garlic, crushed

Mix all ingredients.

Tortellini in Balsamic Vinaigrette

Three-Cheese Tortellini

1 package (7 ounces) dried cheese-filled
  tortellini
¼ cup margarine or butter (½ stick)
½ cup chopped green bell pepper
2 shallots, finely chopped
1 clove garlic, finely chopped
¼ cup all-purpose flour
¼ teaspoon pepper
1¾ cups milk
½ cup shredded mozzarella cheese
  (2 ounces)
½ cup shredded Swiss cheese (2 ounces)
¼ cup grated Parmesan or Romano
  cheese

Cook tortellini as directed on package; drain.
Heat margarine in 3-quart saucepan over medium heat. Cook bell pepper, shallots and garlic
in margarine about 3 minutes. Stir in flour and
pepper. Cook, stirring constantly, until mixture is
bubbly; remove from heat. Stir in milk. Heat to
boiling, stirring constantly. Boil and stir 1 minute;
remove from heat. Stir in mozzarella and Swiss
cheeses until melted. Add tortellini and stir until
coated. Sprinkle with Parmesan cheese.

5 servings

PER SERVING: Calories 390; Protein 16 g; Carbohydrate 41 g; Fat 18 g; Cholesterol 30 mg; Sodium 300 mg

Macaroni and Cheese with Green Chiles

2 cups uncooked shell macaroni (about
  8 ounces)
½ cup milk
½ cup shredded Cheddar cheese
  (2 ounces)
½ cup chopped red bell pepper or 1 jar
  (2 ounces) diced pimientos, drained
¼ cup sliced pitted ripe olives
1 can (4 ounces) chopped green chiles,
  drained
½ teaspoon salt

Cook macaroni as directed on package; drain.
Stir in remaining ingredients. Cook over low heat
about 5 minutes, stirring occasionally, until
cheese is melted and sauce is hot.

4 servings

PER SERVING: Calories 305; Protein 12 g; Carbohydrate 49 g; Fat 7 g; Cholesterol 15 mg; Sodium 1000 mg

Pita Pizzas

4 whole wheat pita breads (4 inches in
   diameter)
1 small onion, chopped (about ¼ cup)
1 small clove garlic, finely chopped
1 can (15½ ounces) great northern
   beans, drained and liquid reserved
2 tablespoons chopped fresh or 2 teaspoons dried basil leaves
¼ teaspoon salt
1 large tomato, seeded and cut into
   ¼-inch pieces
1 large green bell pepper, cut into 16 thin
   rings
1 cup shredded part-skim mozzarella
   cheese (4 ounces)

Heat oven to 425°. Split each pita bread in half
around edge with knife. Place in ungreased jelly
roll pan, 15½ × 10½ × 1 inch. Bake uncovered
about 5 minutes or just until crisp. Cook onion
and garlic in reserved bean liquid in 10-inch nonstick skillet over medium heat about 5 minutes,
stirring occasionally. Stir in beans; heat through.

Place bean mixture, basil and salt in blender or
food processor. Cover and blend or process until
smooth. Spread about 2 tablespoons bean mixture on each pita bread half. Top each with tomato, bell pepper and cheese. Bake 5 to 7
minutes or until cheese is melted.

4 servings

PER SERVING: Calories 320; Protein 21 g; Carbohydrate 45 g; Fat 6 g; Cholesterol 15 mg; Sodium 680 mg

Swiss Cheese Fondue

*Fondue—the word is French for
"melted"—is quintessentially Swiss. This
dish is great fun—dipping, dunking and los-
ing bread!*

2 cups shredded natural (not processed)
   Swiss cheese (8 ounces)
2 cups shredded Gruyère cheese
   (8 ounces)
1 tablespoon cornstarch
1 clove garlic, cut into halves
1 cup dry white wine or chicken broth
1 tablespoon lemon juice
3 tablespoons kirsch or dry sherry or
   chicken broth
½ teaspoon salt
⅛ teaspoon white pepper
French bread, cut into 1-inch cubes

Toss cheeses with cornstarch until coated. Rub
garlic on bottom and side of heavy saucepan or
skillet; add wine. Heat over low heat just until
bubbles rise to surface (wine should not boil).
Stir in lemon juice.

Gradually add cheeses, about ½ cup at a time,
stirring constantly with wooden spoon over low
heat until cheeses are melted. Stir in kirsch, salt
and white pepper. Remove to earthenware fondue dish; keep warm over low heat. Spear bread
cubes with fondue forks; dip and swirl in fondue
with stirring motion. If fondue becomes too thick,
stir in ¼ to ½ cup heated wine.

4 servings

PER SERVING: Calories 570; Protein 36 g; Carbohy-
drates 34 g; Fat 32 g; Cholesterol 100 mg; Sodium 830 mg

NOTE. An additional 2 cups shredded Swiss
cheese can be substituted for the Gruyère
cheese.

Baked Apple and Cheese Pancake

Baked Apple and Cheese Pancake

¼ cup margarine or butter (½ stick)
1 cup all-purpose flour
1 cup milk
½ teaspoon salt
4 eggs
1 cup shredded Swiss, white Cheddar or Monterey Jack cheese (4 ounces)
½ lemon
2 medium apples or pears, thinly sliced
Powdered sugar

Heat oven to 425°. Heat margarine in rectangular pan, 13 × 9 × 2 inches, in oven until hot and bubbly. Beat flour, milk, salt and eggs until well blended. Pour into pan.

Bake until sides of pancake are puffed and deep golden brown, 20 to 25 minutes. Sprinkle with cheese. Squeeze juice from lemon over apples; arrange in center of pancake. Sprinkle with powdered sugar.   **4 servings**

PER SERVING: Calories 480; Protein 20 g; Carbohydrate 42 g; Fat 26 g; Cholesterol 245 mg; Sodium 570 mg

Bean and Cheese Tacos

Serve these meatless soft tacos with your favorite salsa.

1 can (8 ounces) kidney beans, drained and liquid reserved
1 clove garlic, finely chopped
4 flour tortillas (8 inches in diameter)
1 cup part-skim ricotta cheese (8 ounces)
¼ cup grated Parmesan cheese
¼ cup chopped green onions (with tops)
1 tablespoon chopped fresh or 1 teaspoon dried cilantro leaves

Heat oven to 350°. Mash beans and garlic. (Add 1 to 2 tablespoons reserved bean liquid if beans are dry.) Place tortillas on ungreased cookie sheet. Spread about ¼ cup of the bean mixture on half of each tortilla to within ½ inch of edge. Mix cheeses, onions and cilantro; spread over beans. Fold tortillas over filling.

Bake about 10 minutes or until tortillas begin to brown and filling is hot.   **4 servings**

PER SERVING: Calories 195; Protein 12 g; Carbohydrate 22 g; Fat 7 g; Cholesterol 20 mg; Sodium 370 mg

METRIC CONVERSION GUIDE

U.S. UNITS	CANADIAN METRIC	AUSTRALIAN METRIC
Volume		
1/4 teaspoon	1 mL	1 ml
1/2 teaspoon	2 mL	2 ml
1 teaspoon	5 mL	5 ml
1 tablespoon	15 mL	20 ml
1/4 cup	50 mL	60 ml
1/3 cup	75 mL	80 ml
1/2 cup	125 mL	125 ml
2/3 cup	150 mL	170 ml
3/4 cup	175 mL	190 ml
1 cup	250 mL	250 ml
1 quart	1 liter	1 liter
1 1/2 quarts	1.5 liter	1.5 liter
2 quarts	2 liters	2 liters
2 1/2 quarts	2.5 liters	2.5 liters
3 quarts	3 liters	3 liters
4 quarts	4 liters	4 liters
Weight		
1 ounce	30 grams	30 grams
2 ounces	55 grams	60 grams
3 ounces	85 grams	90 grams
4 ounces (1/4 pound)	115 grams	125 grams
8 ounces (1/2 pound)	225 grams	225 grams
16 ounces (1 pound)	455 grams	500 grams
1 pound	455 grams	1/2 kilogram

Measurements		Temperatures	
Inches	Centimeters	Fahrenheit	Celsius
1	2.5	32°	0°
2	5.0	212°	100°
3	7.5	250°	120°
4	10.0	275°	140°
5	12.5	300°	150°
6	15.0	325°	160°
7	17.5	350°	180°
8	20.5	375°	190°
9	23.0	400°	200°
10	25.5	425°	220°
11	28.0	450°	230°
12	30.5	475°	240°
13	33.0	500°	260°
14	35.5		
15	38.0		

NOTE
The recipes in this cookbook have not been developed or tested using metric measures. When converting recipes to metric, some variations in quality may be noted.

Index

═══════════════ ◼ ═══════════════

Almond Chicken, 25

Baked Apple and Cheese Pancakes, 75
Bean(s)
  Chile, Picante Pork, 19
  Pizzas, Pita, 73
  Salad, Tuna–, 52
  Tacos, and Cheese, 75
Beef
  Burger(s)
    Bar, 6
    Chile, 6
    with Mushrooms and Onions, Broiled, 6
    Soup, 12
    Teriyaki, Grilled, 6
  Curried, with Fruit, 3
  Dinner, Quick, 4
  Hamburger Skillet, Double-Cheese, 4
  Hot Dish, Easy, 4
  Kabobs, Grilled Meatball, 12
  Lasagne, Quick, 8
  London, Broil, 1
  Sauce, Spaghetti and, 5
  Stir-Fry, –Orange, 3
  Stroganoff, Ground Beef, 13
  Sweet and Sour, 1
  Tacos, Easy, 8
  Tips
    Burger Bar, 6
    Storage, Freezing and Defrosting, Ground Meat, 10
Blue Cheese Omelet with Pears, 67
Broccoli
  Chicken with, Spicy, 26
  Frittata, and Swiss Cheese, 69
  Pasta Shells with Chicken and, 32

Scallops with, and Mushrooms, 57
Broiled
  Burgers with Mushrooms and Onions, 5
  Burgers, Teriyaki, 6
  Kabobs, Meatball, 12
  Pork Chops and Onions, 16
Brown Sauce, 69
Burger(s). *See also* Beef
  Bar, 6
  Chile, 6
  Hamburger Skillet, Double-Cheese, 4
  with Mushrooms and Onions, Broiled, 5
  Soup, Beef, 12
  Teriyaki, Grilled, 6

Catfish, Cornmeal fried, 41
Cheese
  Egg(s) and, Quick, 65
  Fondue, Swiss, 73
  Hamburger Skillet, Double-, 4
  Lasagne, Quick, 8
  Macaroni and, with Green Chiles, 72
  Pancake, Baked Apple and, 75
  Tacos, Bean and, 75
  Tortellini, Three-, 70
Chicken
  Breast(s)
    Almond, 25
    Barbecued, Oriental, 25
    with Broccoli, Spicy, 26
    Kabobs, Peanutty, 28
    Lemon, 25
    in Lemon-Caper Sauce, 23
    and Nectarines, Curried, 30
    in Mustard Sauce, 23

Sandwiches, Open-Face Pita, 28
  Stir-Fry, –Chutney, 26
  Waldorf, 30
  Curry, Easy, 31
  Pasta Shells with, and Broccoli, 32
  Pasta, Tarragon and, 32
  Salad
    Mexican, 34
    Oriental, 33
    Raspberry–, 31
    Thighs, Curried, 31
Chile, Picante Pork, 19
Chile Burgers, 6
Chutney Dressing, Trout and Spinach Salad with, 51
Crawfish Étouffée, 54
Curry(ied)
  Beef with Fruit, 3
  Chicken
    Easy, 31
    and Nectarines, 30
    Thighs, 31
  Eggs and Vegetables on Rice, 70
  Scallops, 57

Dilled Cucumbers, Salmon with, 46
Dilled Pasta Salad with Smoked Fish, 51
Double-Cheese Hamburger Skillet, 4
Dressing. *See* Salad

Easy Hot Dish, 4
Easy Tacos, 8
Egg(s)
  Curried, and Vegetables on Rice, 70
  Festival, 64

Egg(s) *(cont.)*
Florentine, 65
Foo Yong, 69
Frittata, Broccoli and Swiss
Cheese, 69
Frittata, Vegetable, 68
Huevos Rancheros, 64
Omelet(s)
Bacon and Gruyère, Rolled, 20
Blue Cheese, with Pears, 67
Ham and Gruyère, Rolled, 20
Malaysian, 68
Sausage and Gruyère, Rolled,
20
Tips, 67
Vegetable and Ham, 22
Poached, 65
Quick, and Cheese, 65
Roulade, Ham, 47
Roulade, Smoked Salmon, 47
Scrambled, Home-style, 63
Southwestern, 63

Fajitas, Southwest Turkey, 38
Festival Eggs, 64
Fish. *See also* Seafood
Catfish, Cornmeal-fried, 41
Coatings, Quick, 42
Fillets with Green Peppers and
Mushrooms, 42
Halibut, Oven-poached, 49
Mahimahi in Fennel Sauce, 44
Microwaving, 46
Oven-fried, 41
Oriental, with Bok Choy, 43
Red Snapper, Spicy Breaded, 42
Salad
Pasta, with Smoked Fish,
Dilled, 51
Trout and Spinach, with Chut-
ney Dressing, 51
Tuna–Bean, 52
Salmon
with Dilled cucumbers, 46
Hash, 47
Roulade, Smoked, 47
Steaks with Asparagus and
Peas, 44
Salsa, 43
Sea Bass with Green Beans, 49
Sole, Mediterranean-style, 48
Sole with Red Grapes, 48
Tuna Steaks, Gingered, 48–49
Fondue, Swiss Cheese, 73
Frittata, Broccoli and Swiss
Cheese, 69
Frittata, Vegetable, 68
Fruit
Beef with, Curried, 3
Chicken and Nectarines, Curried,
30
Chicken Salad, Rapsberry–, 31

Omelet with Pears, Blue Cheese,
67
Pork with Peaches, Gingered, 18
Sole with Red Grapes, 48

Gingered
Pork with Peaches, 16
Tuna Steaks, 48–49
Glazed Turkey Tenderloins, 34
Great Pasta Salads, 61
Grilled
Teriyaki Burgers, 6
Kabob(s)
Meatball, 12
Shrimp and Scallop, 54
Ground
Lamb Kabobs, 15
Beef Stroganoff, 13
Lamb Stroganoff, 13

Ham. *See also* Pork
Omelet, Rolled, and Gruyère, 20
Omelet and, Vegetable, 22
Roulade, 47
and Zucchini with Poppy Seeds,
20
Hash, Salmon, 47
Home-style Scrambled Eggs, 63
Huevos Rancheros, 64

Italian-style Turkey Patties, 38

Jambalaya, Quick, 56

Kabob(s)
Beef, Ground, 15
Chicken, Peanutty, 28
Lamb, Ground, 15
Meatball, Grilled, 12
Shrimp and Scallop, Grilled, 54

Lamb
Chops with Pineapple, 13
Kabobs, Ground, 15
Stroganoff, Ground, 13
with Yogurt-Mint Sauce, 15
Lasagne, Quick, 8
Lemon Chicken, 25
London Broil, 1

Macaroni and Cheese with Chiles,
72
Mahimahi in Fennel Sauce, 44
Malaysian Omelet, 68
Mediterranean-style, Sole, 48
Mexican Chicken Salad, 34
Microwaving Fish, 46
Mushroom(s)
Burgers with, and Onions,
Broiled, 5
Fish Fillets with Green Peppers
and, 42

Scallops with Broccoli and, 57
Mussels in Wine Sauce, Steamed,
61
Mustard Sauce, Chicken Breasts in,
23

Noodle(s). *See also* Pasta
Dish, Easy Hot, 4
Hamburger Skillet, Double-
Cheese, 4
Salad, Oriental Chicken, 33
Soup, Burger Beef, 12

Omelet(s). *See also* Egg(s)
Bacon and Gruyère, Rolled, 20
Blue Cheese, with Pears, 67
Ham and Gruyère, Rolled, 20
Malaysian, 68
Sausage and Gruyère, Rolled,
20
Tips, 67
Vegetable and Ham, 22
Open-Face Pita Sandwiches, 28
Oriental
Barbecued Chicken, 25
Chicken Salad, 33
Fish with Bok Choy, 43
Oven-fried Fish, 41
Oven-poached Halibut, 49

Pasta. *See also* Noodle(s)
Chicken, Tarragon and, 32
Cooking Timetable, 33
Fettuccine, Veal with Spinach
and, 10
Lasagne, Quick, 8
Macaroni and Cheese with Green
Chiles, 72
Primavera, Turkey–, 39
Salad(s)
Great, 61
with Smoked Fish, Dilled, 51
Seafood, Tarragon–, 61
Tortellini in Balsamic Vinai-
grette, 70
Turkey–, 39
Shells with Chicken and Broccoli,
32
Spaghetti and Beef Sauce, 5
Tortellini, Three-Cheese, 72
Peanutty Chicken Kabobs, 28
Picante Pork Chile, 19
Pineapple, Lamb Chops with, 13
Pita
Pizzas, 73
Sandwiches, Open-Face, 28
Pork. *See also* Ham
Chile, Picante, 19
Chops and Onions, Broiled, 16
Chops with Rhubarb Sauce, 16
with Garlic-Cream Sauce, Ses-
ame, 18

with Peaches, Gingered, 18
Risotto, and Broccoli, 19

Quick
  Beef Dinner, 4
  Coatings (fish), 42
  Changes for Pasta and Rice, 26
  Eggs and Cheese, 65
  Jambalaya, 56
  Lasagne, 8

Raspberry–Chicken Salad, 31
Rice
  Eggs and Vegetables on, Curried,
    70
  Jambalaya, Quick, 56
  Risotto, Pork and Broccoli, 19
Rolled
  Bacon and Gruyère Omelet, 20
  Ham and Gruyère Omelet, 20
  Sausage and Gruyère Omelet, 20

Salad(s)
  Chicken
    Mexican, 34
    Oriental, 33
    Raspberry–, 31
    South Seas, 52
  Dressing
    Balsamic Vinaigrette, 70
    Chutney, 51
    Ginger, 33
    Raspberry, 31
  Pasta
    Great, 61
    with Smoked Fish, Dilled, 51
    Tortellini in Balsamic Vinai-
      grette, 70
    Turkey–, 39
  Seafood, Tarragon–, 61
  Shrimp, South Seas, 52
  Trout and Spinach with Chutney
    Dressing, 51
  Tuna–Bean, 52
Salmon
  with Dilled Cucumbers, 46
  Hash, 47
  Roulade, Smoked, 47
  Steaks with Asparagus and Peas,
    44
Salsa Fish, 43
Sandwiches, Open-Face Pita, 28
Sandwich, Turkey Oven, 36
Sauce(s)
  Beef, Spaghetti and, 5
  Fennel, Mahimahi in, 44
  Garlic-Cream, Sesame Pork with,
    18
  Lemon-Caper, Chicken Breasts
    in, 23

Mustard, Chicken Breasts in, 23
Rhubarb, Pork Chops with, 16
Wine, Steamed Mussels in, 61
Yogurt-Mint, Lamb with, 15
Sausage and Gruyère Omelet,
  Rolled, 20
Scallop(s)
  with Broccoli and Mushrooms, 57
  Curried, 57
  Kabobs, Grilled Shrimp and, 54
  Stir-fried, and Pea Pods, 59
  in Wine Sauce, 56
Sea Bass with Green Beans, 49
Seafood. See also Fish
  Crabmeat with Celery Cabbage,
    Stir-fried, 59
  Crawfish Étouffée, 54
  Jambalaya, Quick, 56
  Mussels in Wine Sauce,
    Steamed, 61
  Salad, Tarragon–, 61
  Scallops
    with Broccoli and Mushrooms,
      57
    Curried, 57
    Stir-fried, and Pea Pods, 59
    in Wine Sauce, 56
  Shrimp
    Cilantro, 53
    Étouffée, 54
    Fajitas, 53
    Jambalaya, Quick, 56
    Kabobs, Grilled, and Scallops, 54
    Salad, South Seas, 52
Sesame Pork with Garlic-Cream
  Sauce, 18
Shrimp. See also Fish; Seafood
  Cilantro, 53
  Étouffée, 54
  Fajitas, 53
  Jambalaya, Quick, 56
  Kabobs, Grilled, and Scallops, 54
  Salad, South Seas, 52
Sole with Red Grapes, 48
Smoked Salmon Roulade, 47
Soup, Burger Beef, 112
Soup Shortcuts, 22
South Seas Chicken Salad, 52
South Seas Shrimp Salad, 52
Southwest Turkey Fajitas, 38
Southwestern Eggs, 63
Spaghetti and Beef Sauce, 5
Spicy
  Breaded Red Snapper, 42
  Chicken with Broccoli, 26
Spinach
  Trout and, with Chutney Dress-
    ing, 51
  Turkey–Pasta, 39
  Veal with, and Fettuccine, 10

Steamed Mussels in Wine Sauce,
  61
Stir-Fry(ied)
  Beef–Orange, 3
  Chicken–Chutney, 26
  Crabmeat with Celery Cabbage,
    59
  Scallops and Pea Pod, 59
Stroganoff, Ground Lamb, 13
Sweet and Sour Beef, 1
Swiss Cheese Fondue, 73

Tacos, Bean and Cheese, 75
Tacos, Easy, 8
Tarragon and Chicken Pasta, 32
Tarragon-Seafood Salad, 61
Teriyaki Burgers, Grilled, 6
Three-Cheese Tortellini, 72
Tips
  Burger Bar, 6
  Eggs and Cheese, Quick, 65
  Microwaving Fish, 46
  Pasta
    Cooking Timetable, 33
    Quick Changes for, and Rice,
      26
  Salads, Great, 61
  Quick (fish) Coatings, 42
  Soup, Shortcuts, 22
  Storage, Freezing and Defrosting,
    Ground Meat, 10
Tortellini in Balsamic Vinaigrette,
  70
Trout and Spinach Salad with Chut-
  ney Dressing, 51
Tuna–Bean Salad, 52
Tuna Steaks, Gingered, 48–49
Turkey
  Divan, 36
  Fajitas, Southwest, 38
  Oven Sandwich, 36
  –Pasta Primavera, 39
  –Pasta Salad, 39
  Patties, Italian-style, 38
  Slices with Walnuts, 34
  Tenderloins, Glazed, 34

Veal with Spinach and Fettuccine,
  10
Vegetable(s)
  Eggs and, on Rice, Curried, 70
  Frittata, 68
  Omelet, and Ham, 22
  Omelet, Malaysian, 68

Waldorf Chicken, 30
Walnuts, Turkey Slices with, 34

Zucchini, Ham and, with Poppy
  Seeds, 20